LEADERSHIP

LESSONS FROM *Bill Snyder*

LEADERSHIP

LESSONS FROM *Bill Snyder*

Robert J. Shoop
Kansas State University

Susan M. Scott
Kansas State University

AG Press Publishing
Manhattan, Kansas

Cover photo by Peter G. Aiken.

Cover design by Dana D. Smith.

Layout by Lori L. Daniel.

Printed in the United States of America by AG Press, Inc.

ISBN 0-89745-981-4

We dedicate this book to the past, current, and future students in the Leadership Studies program at Kansas State University and to our children: Paul Scott Angle; Allison Shoop; and Sean, Shannon, Meredith, Ross, and Whitney Snyder.

Table of Contents

Foreword

I AM VERY HAPPY and honored to recommend this new book, *Leadership Lessons from Bill Snyder*, by Robert J. Shoop and Susan M. Scott. This is an excellent and well-written book. This book is timely because young people all over Kansas and America are searching for the principles of leadership.

I know of no one that better understands the key ingredients of leadership than Coach Bill Snyder. He has been stressing the qualities and meaning of leadership for over a generation. Bill Snyder not only teaches the principles of leadership every day of the week, he lives by them.

For years and years, Coach Bill Snyder has been articulating to his players and fellow coaches the principles and concepts of hard work and dedication, the setting and meeting of goals, the vital importance of loyalty and integrity, the value of dependability and credibility, and the championing of a caring attitude for fellow student athletes and friends. With this superb book entitled *Leadership Lessons from Bill Snyder*, readers all over America will not only systematically be able to find out exactly what Bill Snyder's leadership principles and values are, but they will be able to apply those lessons and vital truths to their own lives.

Quite frankly, anyone who reads this book from cover to cover will benefit greatly. Readers will find the book inspiring and rewarding. No matter how young or old and no matter what career or profession someone is in, this book will provide clear and common sense values and leadership principles for all who read it.

As President of Kansas State University and a good friend of Coach Bill Snyder, I have known for a long time why he has always been successful. Coach Snyder has the crucial qualities for leadership: the characteristic of vision; the ability to communicate that vision and set of expectations; the innate understanding of why it is important to hire great people and, then, to empower them; the trait of having trust in those around you; the importance of sincerely caring about others; the possession of an iron will and a never-give-up attitude; and the trait of simply outworking everyone else. I have always known this about Bill Snyder. But by reading this book by Robert Shoop and Susan Scott everyone else can know about these qualities of leadership first hand. I highly recommend this book to students, faculty, staff, alumni, and the general public.

Jon Wefald
President, Kansas State University
Manhattan, Kansas

Foreword

*F*OR THE YOUTH OF OUR NATION, this is the most complex and most difficult time in the history of our society. This country is crying out for strong positive leadership for and from its youth. The pathway to success for our nation and future generations is very likely dependent upon the leadership development of today's youth and young adults.

We should recognize the critical need for the development of new leaders to direct this generation toward a value system that will promote morality, integrity, credibility, responsibility, accountability, honesty, hard work, self discipline, and genuine concern for others.

I am honored to contribute to that leadership development through this book and at the same time to assist financially with the Kansas State University Leadership Studies Program, the Student Athlete Leadership Program, and the development of the University's Hale Library.

I encourage those of you in the University's Leadership Studies Program (and each reader) to accept the opportunity and the responsibility to utilize your talents and leadership capacity to impact the lives of our youth.

We ask the players in our football program to first share their lives with those who want to help make their lives better and then commit themselves to helping make the lives of others better. You too can be that someone who wants to make the lives of others better.

Bill Snyder
Head Coach, KSU Football Program
Manhattan, Kansas

Thank You Letter
from 1998 Leadership Studies Graduates

Dear Coach Snyder,

THE FIRST GRADUATING CLASS of the Leadership Studies minor would like to thank you, Coach Snyder, for your commitment to leadership development and for promoting the academic interests of all students at Kansas State University. Your commitment to developing the whole person and organization through attention to detail and relationship building directly correlates with the transformational leadership style we have studied in our courses. *Leadership Lessons from Bill Snyder* will serve as an invaluable resource for students at K-State, as well as for anyone who is interested in becoming a better leader.

We are also grateful that the proceeds from this book will directly benefit undergraduate students and student programs at K-State. We believe that the study of leadership is invaluable to all students and to us as we head into the next stages of our lives. As a complement to the content that a student learns in a major field of study, Leadership Studies provides a base of knowledge in leadership theory and the opportunity to develop the skills necessary to be an effective leader. Leadership Studies involves learning not just what leaders do, but who leaders are, and how they can lead more effectively. We hope to enter the work world not only as competent employees, but as employees with the skills and abilities to be effective leaders.

Each of us left Kansas State University striving to utilize our knowledge of effective leadership theories and put that knowledge into practice in our own lives. Patrick Carney, Renee Fisher, Jonathan Freeman, and Aaron Otto have each gone on to graduate schools in the fields of law (Kansas University), student affairs administration (Michigan State University), medicine (Kansas University), and public administration (George Washington University) respectively. Others will be starting careers in the corporate world. Kate Tirrell will work with Sprint in Kansas City, Missouri; Casey Carlson will work with Deloitt and Touche, LLP, in Boston, Massachusetts; and Peggy Niemann will begin work with The MASTER Teacher in Manhattan, Kansas. Justin Kastner, recipient of Truman and Fulbright scholarships, will be studying overseas and Maggie Keating leads a statewide political campaign in Topeka, Kansas. Lindsay S. Weir has accepted a position at the University of Texas Athletic Department, Austin, Texas, and Aubrey Abbott works with the Leadership Studies program at K-State. Our directions and focus may be different, but wherever we choose to go from here, we will carry with us the knowledge that any person, at any given time, in any given situation, can step forward and exhibit true leadership.

The opportunity to be involved in the development of this book has been a great one. Thank you for the unique opportunity to ask our own questions on leadership. We also appreciate the way Susan and Bob used our capstone course, *Leadership for the 21st Century*, as a sounding board for feedback on the questions that they would be asking you and others interviewed for the book. They also solicited our input regarding the title, cover design, and organization of the book. *Leadership Lessons from Bill Snyder* is truly a product of the collaborative leadership style we have studied in class.

Once again, thank you Coach Snyder, Dr. Shoop, and Dr. Scott for this invaluable tool and resource that you have given to each of us. We truly appreciate all that each of you do for the students of Kansas State University.

Aubrey Abbott	Jonathan Freeman	Peggy Niemann
Casey Carlson	Justin Kastner	Aaron Otto
Patrick Carney	Maggie Keating	Kathryn Tirrell
Renee Fisher		Lindsay S. Weir

Acknowledgments

O UR FIRST THANK YOU goes to Coach Snyder. We are very appreciative of Coach Snyder's willingness to spend a considerable amount of time talking with us about his vision of leadership. Obviously, the book would not exist were it not for his commitment to the students of Kansas State University and to others interested in leadership. Although it is easy to become cynical in this day and age, our time with Coach Snyder was both educational and inspiring. He is the "real deal."

This book is not only the result of the collaboration of Coach Snyder, Susan and Bob, but also the combined efforts of the students in the undergraduate Leadership Studies program; over seventy-five people who contributed their time and talent; and our families. Students in the Leadership Studies program contributed questions that they wanted to ask Coach Snyder, some of which are quoted throughout the book. In addition to giving us their support as we worked on this project, our spouses, Lane Marshall, Kansas State University professor, and Mary Shoop, Washburn University professor, willingly gave of their time and talent to read and comment on the various drafts of the manuscript.

We also thank President Jon Wefald. The "Miracle in Manhattan" could not have happened without the vision and leadership of President Wefald and his administrative staff. President Wefald generously gave many hours of his time, sharing views on leadership and providing background information about the process of enhancing not only the football program, but the entire university.

A sincere thank you is also given to Vice President Robert Krause and Associate Vice President and Dean of Student Life Pat Bosco. Bob was unselfish in sharing his insights into the history of the program, and on leadership in general. Pat Bosco is the driving force behind the Leadership Studies and Student Leadership Development programs at Kansas State University. He also spent a considerable amount of time discussing the conceptualization for this book.

We also wish to thank Joan Friederich, Coach Snyder's secretary and administrative assistant, who was an invaluable part of this project. In addition to assisting us with the transcription of our interviews with Coach Snyder, Joan helped us to contact former players, scheduled meetings and interviews, and most importantly always had an encouraging word and smile. Joan is a dedicated professional and a "mom" to every player in the football program at Kansas State University.

Tom Carlin, General Manager of AG Press, deserves a special thank you. We wrote this book with the goal of making a financial contribution to Hale Library, the Student Athlete Leadership Program, and the Leadership Studies Program. Tom and his partner, Dean Coughenour, agreed to advance the money needed to publish this book. They further agreed to ensure that, after expenses were recovered, 80% of the income from the sales of this book will go to the above mentioned groups. Tom was also instrumental in the conceptualization of the book, and was an enthusiastic supporter of the project from the beginning.

Special thanks are also in order for Max Urick, Director of Athletics, and Kent Brown, Director of Sports Information. Each of these men went above and beyond the call of duty in assisting us with marketing the book. Max also shared many significant insights about athletic administration and leadership in general.

We would also like to thank Jack Hayhow, business leader, Overland Park, Kansas, and Major Steve Dorfman, KSU Air Force ROTC, for reading and commenting on the manuscript.

Jennifer Keller, Sports Information Assistant, and Aubrey Abbott,

Leadership Studies Coordinator, deserve special thanks. Jennifer conducted a number of the interviews with former players, and served as our liaison with the sports information office, as well as reading and commenting on the manuscript. Aubrey assisted with the day-to-day management of the project. She coordinated the manuscript preparation, read and commented on the manuscript, and was always there to assist us with tasks, both large and small. Their professionalism and good cheer were invaluable.

We recognize and are extremely appreciative of the significant commitment made by the following people, each of whom was enthusiastic in their willingness to assist with the development of the book or by sharing personal insights and expertise: Carol Adolph, Ticket Office Manager; Theresa Alexander, KSU football program secretary; Ernie Barrett, Director of Development, KSU athletics; Brooks Barta, football coach and math teacher, Holton, Kansas (linebacker 89-92); Sandy Beisel, business person, Douglass, Kansas; Doug Beisel, teacher and football coach, Douglass, Kansas; Trent Benisch, KSU undergraduate student; Gordon Brown, police officer, KSU (defensive back, 94-95); Curt Brungardt, Director of Leadership Studies, Fort Hays State University, Hays, Kansas; John Butler, funeral director, Hastings, Nebraska (defensive end 89-93); Tom Byers, teacher and football coach, Blue Valley Northwest High School, Olathe, Kansas (free-safety 88-89); Casey Carlson, 1997, 1998 KSU graduate; Patrick Carney, 1998 KSU graduate; Barry Clark, Manhattan attorney; Chris Cobb, sales manager, Dallas, Texas (quarterback 89-90); Tim Colston, KSU student (defensive lineman, 91-96); Vanessa Cushenberry, KSU undergraduate student; Robert DeBruyn, business leader, Manhattan, Kansas; Tracey DeBruyn, business leader, Manhattan, Kansas; Demetric Denmark, KSU student (corner back, 95-97); Amy Donahy, 1998 KSU graduate; Mike "Crash" Ekeler, director of sales and marketing, Omaha, Nebraska (linebacker 92-95); Jim Epps, Senior Associate Director, KSU Intercollegiate Athletics;

Renee Fisher, 1998 KSU graduate; Tim Fitzgerald, Editor and Publisher, *Powercat Illustrated*, Manhattan, Kansas; Cindy Fox, Assistant Athletic Director, KSU Intercollegiate Athletics; Jonathan Freeman, 1998 KSU graduate; Matt Garber, assistant principal and head football coach, Sabetha, Kansas (quarterback 88-92); Rob Goode, business owner, Manhattan, Kansas (linebacker and captain 85-88); Kathy Greene, Director, KSU Educational and Supportive Services; Bill Hall, fly fisherman,

Missoula, Montana; Lyle Hasenbank, Building Supervisor, KSU Vanier Complex; Kye Hittle, KSU undergraduate student; Kirby Hocutt, NCAA Licensing Coordinator, Overland Park, Kansas (linebacker 90-94); Jeremy Hogaboom, KSU undergraduate student; Michael C. Holen, Dean, KSU College of Education; Katha Hurt, elementary school principal, Manhattan, Kansas; Mandy Inlow, KSU undergraduate student; Michael Johnson, KSU undergraduate student; Steve Johnson, business person, Lawrence, Kansas; Justin Kastner, 1998 KSU graduate; Maggie Keating, 1998 KSU graduate; Ryan Kerschen, KSU undergraduate student; Larry Kramer, business person, Emporia, Kansas, and former KSU Assistant Football Coach; Phillip M. Levi, long-term care facility administrator, Manhattan, Kansas; Kevin Lockett, NFL football player, Kansas City Chiefs, Overland Park, Kansas (wide receiver 92-97); Reggie McGowan, Director of KSU Upward Bound; Matt Miller, Graduate Assistant/Offense, KSU Intercollegiate Athletics (quarterback, 92-95); Steve Miller, Global Sports Marketing Director, Nike, Beaverton, Oregon;

Emily Morrison, KSU undergraduate student; Dennis Mullin, business leader, Manhattan, Kansas; Danny Needham, salesman, Dallas, Texas (strong and free safety 88-89); Jennafer Neufeld, 1998 KSU graduate; Quentin Neujahr, NFL football player, Jacksonville Jaguars, Jacksonville, Florida (center 89-93); Peggy Niemann, 1998 KSU graduate; Aaron Otto, 1998 KSU graduate; Kevin R. Page, Director of Academic Affairs, KSU Intercollegiate Athletics; Deb Patterson, Head Women's Basketball Coach, KSU Intercollegiate Athletics; Julie Polson, Department Secretary, Educational Administration and Foundations, KSU College of Education; Mark Porter, business person, Houston, Texas; Leo Prieto, KSU undergraduate student; Kitt Rawlings, assistant football coach, Southwest Missouri State, Springfield, Missouri (running back, corner back, strong safety 90-93); Linda Robinson, business person, Mulvane, Kansas; Mike Scott, business person, Lawrence, Kansas; Pat Scott, teacher and coach, Victoria, Kansas; Greg Sharpe, "Voice of the Wildcats," Topeka, Kansas; Howard Sherwood, business leader, Wichita, Kansas; Angie Shilling, KSU undergraduate student; Allison Shoop, KSU undergraduate student; Michael Smith, Assistant Football Coach, KSU Intercollegiate Athletics; Chris Smither, KSU undergraduate student; Bob Snell, professor and KSU faculty representative to Big 12 athletic conference and NCAA; Sean Snyder, Associate Director, KSU Intercollegiate Athletics; Veryl Switzer, Associate Director, Intercollegiate Athletics; Mordean Taylor-Archer;

KSU Associate Provost for Diversity and Dual Career Development; Tim Taylor, KSU undergraduate student; Donna Thomas, KSU secretary; David Thompson, KSU Professor and Department Head, Educational Administration and Leadership, College of Education; Kathryn Tirrell, 1998 KSU graduate; Laird Veatch, Director of Annual Giving, University of Missouri Athletics, Columbia, Missouri (linebacker 90-94); Stan Weber, business leader, Overland Park, Kansas; Verneta White, KSU undergraduate student; and Lindsay S. Weir, 1998 KSU graduate.

A special note of appreciation from Susan goes to her father, Bob Scott, "who is the original model of caring leadership, in our family and in his work." A special note of appreciation from Bob goes to Jim Shoop, his father, who led by example and taught him about honesty and courage.

Preface

W E CAME TO COACH SNYDER with a proposal. To understand what we wanted requires that we begin our story in February 1998. Kansas State University was hosting the 10th Annual High School Leadership Conference. Over 300 spirited, committed and bright high school students were just finishing eating their lunches in the ballroom of K-State Student Union. The morning workshops had proven this group to be inquisitive, intense, and a bit rowdy. When Coach Snyder was introduced as the featured lunch speaker he was greeted by a standing ovation. We watched, a bit surprised, that a college football coach whose demeanor was so reserved commanded such respect from this audience. It was evident that everyone in attendance, from those who belonged to the Future Farmers of America to the 60's wannabes, were eager to hear Snyder speak. As the rowdiness in the room subsided, we settled in to listen. We were treated to an uncommon experience. Coach Snyder spoke of values, value-based decision-making, and successful goal accomplishment strategies. He was not talking about how to become a successful athlete or coach. He was sharing powerful insights about how to lead.

We have each been teaching and talking about leadership for 20 years and didn't expect to hear much that we hadn't heard before. We were wrong. As Snyder demonstrated his authentic desire to positively impact the lives of his listeners, it became clear that his leadership philosophy is compatible with many well-respected leadership theories and has original and unique leadership lessons for anyone interested in becoming a better student, teacher, parent, business person, or coach.

We are fans of the Kansas State football program, but did not know Coach Snyder personally. As we talked about the leadership components we saw in Coach Snyder, we became convinced that anyone interested in leadership could learn important lessons from him.

We teach in the Leadership Studies program and work with students as they begin to develop their strengths as future employees. Our desire to help these students learn about leadership combined with Coach Snyder's experience as a leader led to the vision of this book.

Coach Snyder agreed to meet with us and discuss our idea. As he welcomed us into his office, he paused in the hallway to conclude a conversation. As we waited the few moments for our meeting to begin, our eyes naturally wandered around the room. Although he has hundreds of pictures and mementos that he could use to decorate his office, there are surprisingly few photos. There is a picture of Mrs. Snyder and their children. On the wall directly to his right is a large, beautifully framed production cell from the cartoon *Pinocchio*. Additionally, there is an item at the center of his desk that he must look at a hundred times a day — a Lucite plaque with a quote etched into it. The plaque is not positioned for the benefit of his visitor, but is placed where Coach Snyder will see it each time he sits at his desk. It reads:

Persistence

Nothing in the world can take the place of persistence. Talent will not; nothing is more common than unsuccessful men with talent. Genius will not; unrewarded genius is almost a proverb. Education will not; the world is full of educated derelicts. Persistence and determination alone are omnipotent. The slogan "Press On" has solved and always will solve the problems of the human race.

Calvin Coolidge
President of the United States
1923-29

In that first meeting we talked about the new Leadership Studies program at Kansas State. Coach Snyder was particularly interested in how this book could be used to help students learn about leadership. The three of us decided that the book would take the form of conversations with Coach Snyder on a variety of leadership topics. We worked together to identify some of the lessons that he incorporates into his coaching style.

Background of Leadership Studies

With the publication in 1978 of *Leadership* by James McGregor Burns, a noted political scientist, Leadership Studies began receiving recognition as an academic discipline. In March 1997, the Kansas Board of Regents approved an interdisciplinary Leadership Studies minor for Kansas State University. This minor is offered through the College of Education and was developed by a committee representing every college of the university, practitioners of leadership, and undergraduate students.

Within the first year, the Leadership Studies program experienced substantial enrollment growth and student interest. Coach Snyder's beliefs and practices are quite compatible with the mission of the Leadership Studies program, which is to "Develop knowledgeable, ethical, and caring leaders for a diverse world."

The Leadership Studies program and this book are based upon the following beliefs:

1) Leadership can be taught and learned;

2) Leadership is a process, not a title or position;

3) Leadership is collaborative. As the adage goes, "If you're leading but no one is following, you're really just out for a walk"; and

4) People are not truly leaders if they can only "do" leadership with people who are just like themselves. The ability to communicate across ages, cultures, genders, and socioeconomic backgrounds is essential.

There are many definitions of leadership. However, we believe the one developed by author Joseph Rost is the most usable. He defines leadership as "an influence relationship among leaders and followers who intend real organizational or societal changes that reflect their mutual purposes." As a result, when we examine leadership we look at influence, relationships, change, and mutual purposes.

If this book was about the leadership lessons of a corporate executive, or a financial expert, or a military leader, the examples would be grounded in the world of business, finance, or the military. Because this book is about the leadership lessons of a football coach, the examples, applications, and focus of much of the discussion will be on the football program at Kansas State University. We invite each reader to join us in continually translating these lessons to your individual circumstance. Of course, there are some things about a football program that make it a unique situation. However, a significant portion of what Snyder has implemented in his program can be applied to a wide variety of situations.

It is inspiring to see that a leader can care as much about the athletes and the students as Snyder does, and still have the success that others outside the program look for. He wins games as well as helps people develop. Competitive sports can be a training ground for both positive and negative characteristics. Coach Snyder's method is one that student athletes, as well as readers of this book, can easily understand, learn, and apply in their own lives.

Devotion to his family, an unswerving dedication to helping young people, an ability to focus on his goals, and the commitment to exert the effort necessary to accomplish the task at hand are major themes of Coach Snyder's leadership philosophy.

This book examines these various facets of Snyder's leadership philosophy, and identifies and discusses specific examples of how his philosophy is translated into practice.

James McGregor Burns wrote, "We know all too much about our leaders, but far too little about leadership." Scholars and popular authors continue to call for an end to the dearth of leadership. By joining us in reflecting on how Coach Snyder leads, we can each become better leaders.

Robert J. Shoop and Susan M. Scott
Manhattan, Kansas
August, 1998

About the Format of the Book

Throughout the book, Coach Snyder's words are indicated by italics. The direct quotes of others are enclosed in quotation marks. The questions asked by leadership students are identified by a "?." All other text are the words of the authors.

The book is organized around 20 lessons which are clustered around six themes: Vision and Goal Attainment; Equity, Diversity, and Ethics; Communication; Community; Credibility; and Day-to-Day Management. Each lesson is followed by a conversation with Coach Snyder. The lessons are then supported with examples illustrating how each lesson is actually implemented.

Leadership Lessons from Bill Snyder

Leadership Lesson Number One: Goal attainment is a three-step process: a) significant goals are set based on priorities/values; b) a well-constructed plan is put into place; and c) a "just do it" attitude is adopted.

Leadership Lesson Number Two: A vision of the desired transformation must be established before implementing the goal attainment process.

Leadership Lesson Number Three: Goal attainment is always a balance between a focus on long range-goals and daily improvement.

Leadership Lesson Number Four: The ultimate goal of leadership is continuous improvement, rather than a quantifiable outcome.

Leadership Lesson Number Five: Decision making is: a) conscious and based on established values and priorities; b) participatory within well-defined limits; and c) occasionally intuitive.

Leadership Lesson Number Six: Treating everyone equally while respecting individual differences, needs, and motivations is the key to fairness.

Leadership Lesson Number Seven: Respect for diversity is best achieved by ensuring that everyone is focusing on a common goal.

Leadership Lesson Number Eight: Discriminatory attitudes, behaviors, or statements have no place in an ethical and fair organization and will negatively impact the successful attainment of goals.

Leadership Lesson Number Nine: Ethical organizations are based on loyalty and service to individual members, as well as to the greater community.

Leadership Lesson Number Ten: All communication should be open, direct, and positive.

Leadership Lesson Number Eleven: Successful communication is accomplished through continual repetition of an individualized message.

Leadership Lesson Number Twelve: It is important to explain in detail the reason behind decisions and directives, if possible.

Leadership Lesson Number Thirteen: Storytelling and providing visual images are effective means of communication and leadership.

Leadership Lesson Number Fourteen: A sense of family is important in the organization. Each individual and every task should be valued by every member of the organization.

Leadership Lesson Number Fifteen: Sincere interest and concern must be regularly demonstrated to each member of the organization.

Leadership Lesson Number Sixteen: Integrity, honesty, and trustworthiness are the leader's most important attributes.

Leadership Lesson Number Seventeen: Credibility is earned and established over time.

Leadership Lesson Number Eighteen: A standard of excellence can only be established and maintained by hard work and role modeling.

Leadership Lesson Number Nineteen: Attention to detail and consistency are essential to transforming an organization's climate, and necessary for the continual improvement of the organization.

Leadership Lesson Number Twenty: Managing time, stress, and emotions are learnable leadership skills. The need for these skills increases as the demands of leadership increase.

Prologue

"Miracle in Manhattan"

HEN SPORTS HISTORIANS look back on the 1990's, the Kansas State University football story will undoubtedly be heralded as the "Miracle in Manhattan." The last decade of the twentieth century, and beyond, will be known as the "Bill Snyder Era." They will write about the championships and the bowl games. They will remember that he orchestrated the greatest turnaround in college football history. They will acknowledge that he enhanced the honor of the university and energized an entire state. However, historians will miss an important part of the story if they focus only on Bill Snyder's legacy as a football coach. Snyder is an agent of change and a leader of the first magnitude. Today our society needs competent, capable, caring, ethical leaders at all levels. Coach Snyder is such a leader, but just as importantly he is actively engaged in the process of preparing future leaders.

Before we go any further we should note that Coach Snyder is tired of hearing about what happened before he arrived at Kansas State University. To his way of thinking, the losing records, the declining attendance, and the jokes have nothing to do with him, his coaches or the current players at Kansas State University. We agree. However, in order to understand the significance of what Coach Snyder and his staff have accomplished, and see the effectiveness of his leadership, it is necessary to at least glance at Kansas State football prior to the Snyder Era. This is important because what Snyder has done is much more than what is recorded on the sports pages. It is natural to count up wins, bowl appearances, and All-Americans and think you understand the Kansas State University football program. It is easy to think of the players as gladiators, suited in armor and engaged in war. But, a part of the story that is just as important and often overlooked is that the football team consists of 120 young men who have names and faces, and who will take the lessons they learn on the football field into their futures.

To truly understand the magnitude of the change that has taken place, we need to look at the program prior to Coach Snyder's arrival in Manhattan. Kansas State football had reached rock bottom in 1988. Rob Goode, a captain on that year's team, remembers those days:

> It was pretty bad. Our coach had bailed out on us. He told us halfway through the season that he was quitting. The morale of the players and the coaches was terrible. Players did not

wear their letter jackets or K-State sweats. Being a football player at K-State wasn't something to be proud of. It was common for players to arrive late to meetings and practices. There was no discipline on the team. No one believed we could win.

Before games the head coach would tell the team, "OK let's not get anybody hurt. Let's try to be as competitive as we can. Be careful out there." Imagine what this does to a player getting ready to take the field. Some of the coaches were as undisciplined as the players. For example, during my senior year we were playing Tulane, and were ahead by four points with less than two minutes to play. The defense went back out on the field, but the coaches thought the game was won. They left the coaching box. The players had to go on the field with no coaches to call the defenses. We had a couple pass interference calls and then had twelve men on the field. Tulane went down the field and scored on the last play of the game.

The Toughest Job in the Country

The debacle at Kansas State was a national laughingstock. Coaching at Kansas State had been a "real career stopper." No K-State coach since World War II had gone on to a better coaching job. Perhaps the low point came when an article in the August 1989 issue of *Sports Illustrated* chronicled that in the period between 1946 and 1989 Kansas State had only four winning seasons. The article went on to report, "Kansas State ranks last in the nation in scoring offense and last in scoring defense, and since 1954 last in total offense." In 1988, only 2,700 students bought season tickets. When the then Director of Athletics, Steve Miller, hired Bill Snyder in November of 1988 he told him, "Kansas State is flat on its back. You must have heard it's one of the toughest jobs in the country. It's not. It's *the* toughest."

Less than ten years later, Kansas State University's football program is making a habit of annually winning nine to eleven games and challenging for the conference title. The 1997 team was the fifth in a row to play in a major bowl game. Bill Snyder is now nationally recognized as orchestrating the greatest turnaround in college football history. Greg Sharpe, the radio "Voice of the Wildcats," reports that "Kansas State is one of only six football programs in the nation to win at least nine games in each of the past five seasons. Only Florida State, Florida, Nebraska, Penn State and Ohio State can also make that claim. During that five-year run, the Cats have been ranked in the top twenty-five programs in the nation for fifty-one consecutive weeks." Kansas State has firmly entrenched itself as a perennial college football powerhouse. In 1997 they earned their first-ever berth in one of the prestigious Alliance bowls.

Snyder's unprecedented success at Kansas State hasn't gone unnoticed. He has been named the National Coach of the Year on two occasions and was named Big Eight Coach of the Year three times in a four-year period. In 1996, he was named the Big 12 Coach of the Year. Perhaps former Colorado head coach Bill McCartney said it best: "I don't think anybody has approximated what he has done. I don't think that anybody in college football can compare to what they have done in Manhattan. It looks like the entire university has gotten behind him. They're hitting on all cylinders in recruiting, academically, and in their cohesiveness."

Paul Pasqualoni, head coach at Syracuse, echoed McCartney when he said prior to the Fiesta Bowl, "I don't know of anyone in college football, or football in general, who has done the job of coaching in the 90's that Coach Snyder and his staff have done." Pasqualoni reports that not only does he admire Coach Snyder for what he has done in coaching, but he admires him for what he stands for.

Kansas State's convincing 17-point victory over Big East Champion Syracuse in the 1998 Fiesta Bowl is a good place to begin to understand what Bill Snyder's leadership philosophy is all about. As the final gun sounded, the Kansas State fans went wild. Fans and some players were crying and hugging each other. Vice president Bob Krause echoed the sentiments of many: "It brought tears to my eyes. There was an incredible impact of realizing how far this program had come and what this meant for the university."

A huge party was ready to begin. Amid the noise and the waving banners we looked at Coach Snyder's face. His expression, as he was being hoisted onto the shoulders of several of his players, was not what you might think. We have all come to expect to see winning coaches, particularly after important games, jamming their fists into the air and shouting, or in some cases, spinning around and jumping up and down. Coach Snyder had what can only be described as a bemused expression on his face. It seemed to say, "I am happy that we won, but there is more to come."

How did this transformation take place?

According to Dennis Mullin, Manhattan business leader,

> I think the transformation began with Jon Wefald. If Jon hadn't been the type of president he was, we wouldn't have a Bill Snyder. Jon knew that a winning football program could be the core that allows everyone to buy into his commitment to enhancing the total university. He understood how integral sports are to the university's success. Because of the winning football program, the whole attitude toward Kansas State has improved.

Ernie Barrett, Director of Development of the KSU Athletic Department, first enrolled at Kansas State in 1947, and has been a close observer of its football program. He has more than earned the title of "Mr. K-State." Although past administrations had not made a very strong commitment to football, he always believed that Kansas State could, "win football games." But, he knew it would take a coming together of all the elements at the same time.

All the elements came together in 1988. The previous football coach had resigned and Steve Miller was about to begin what he knew would be a critical job search. In talking about the early stages of the search, Miller said,

> The University was at a crossroads as to whether or not it was going be capable of maintaining its status as a big time university athletically. We had made a lot of progress academically with President Wefald coming in, but athletically, we were definitely in need of an injection of leadership and direction in our football program.
>
> If history has taught us nothing else it has taught us that there are certain leaders at certain times that are absolutely perfect for certain jobs. There are certain leaders that have become extraordinary leaders in certain moments of history,

based upon what the circumstances demanded. Kansas State University required a very special kind of person.

Kansas State conducted a very extensive national search. They wanted someone who understood the state of Kansas and Kansas State University, as well as having the required skills as a football coach. At the conclusion of their interviews, the committee was not satisfied with the fit between the finalists and what was needed at Kansas State.

Associate Athletics Director Jim Epps knew that they needed to find someone who could generate confidence and enthusiasm with the Kansas State fans. They needed somebody who could immediately bond with the team and demonstrate that the staff cared about them as individuals as well as athletes. And last, but not least, they needed someone who knew what it took to win in a very competitive conference. Epps recalls that,

> We were all getting frustrated. It occurred to me that, rather than thinking about an individual, perhaps we needed to be thinking about a program. A program that had gone on the skids and was resurrected. I immediately thought about the University of Iowa.
>
> When Hayden Fry and Bill Snyder were hired at Iowa, a once proud football program was just abysmal. Prior to their arrival, Iowa had seventeen consecutive losing seasons. Fry and his people went in there and turned it around. Not only did they get it going, but they kept it on a very high level. Bill Snyder caught my eye. I noticed that all of Iowa's Big 10 offensive records were established while Snyder was the offensive coordinator.

Miller decided to reopen the search.

> In our first conversation we were on the phone for an hour and a half. He only asked a few questions about the football team. He wanted to know about administrative support, community support, and the kind of support staff that was available for the program. He asked about the academic counseling pro-

gram and about the attitude of the faculty toward the football program. We were incredibly impressed with his seriousness and his overall demeanor.

Miller went to Iowa to meet with Snyder. He remembers that Snyder was,

> . . . Very happy at the University of Iowa. He was reluctant to come, not because he did not think he could win at Kansas State, but because he did not know if Kansas State University was as committed as he was. The interview process was very interesting in that he interviewed me as much or more as I interviewed him. A major portion of his ultimate decision to come to Kansas State was us convincing Bill that we were going to provide him with what he needed to be successful. This was not so much in terms of dollars and cents as it was in terms of human commitment.

The search committee consisted of faculty, administrators, community leaders, and prominent boosters. When the committee came out of their interview it was clear that they were very impressed. Bob Snell, the faculty representative to the NCAA and Big 12 Conference, said "This is the guy, you can shut the search down, he is head and shoulders above anyone else we have talked to. He is really a unique and impressive fellow."

People who were involved in the search process frequently mention that Snyder came across more like a professor than a football coach. They were not only impressed with his style, but more importantly by his substance. One of the most unique references came from Bo Schembechler, then head coach at the University of Michigan, who said, "Get him the hell out of the Big Ten."

His work ethic and the way he approached problems convinced Miller and others that he was the right person for the job. They were particularly impressed by his unflappability. They could see that he was a person that would not become confused or upset, no matter what happened.

The process of negotiation was not about his compensation, but about the compensation of his assistant coaches. Everyone at Kansas State was impressed by Snyder's obviously sincere concern about the people around him. As with any any great leader, Snyder knew that he would require assistance and institutional support. He did not feel that Kansas State would have a chance to succeed without a total commitment from those in authority. He wanted to know what that commitment was.

The Right People at the Right Time

Fortunately, the right people were in the right place at the right time. Since taking the helm in 1986, as Kansas State's 12th president, Jon Wefald, has worked with students, faculty, staff, alumni, and friends to move the university forward on every front. Without Wefald's support and encouragement, the football program could not have turned around. When Wefald came to the university it was in a free-fall. It had gone from 19,500 students in 1980 to 17,500 in 1986. Wefald had a vision for Kansas State University that included all areas of the university striving for excellence. According to Provost Jim Coffman, President Wefald "clearly understood that the perception that the football program was in disarray was having a negative impact on the university at large."

No football resurrection would have occurred at Kansas State without the leadership of President Wefald and his administrative staff. Wefald led a total university renaissance. He believed that the raw materials for success were there, but that "we could be so much better." He wanted to get the best people in the right positions. At the same time that money was being raised and spent to increase the assistant coaches' salaries, upgrade the training and learning facilities, and revitalize the stadium, the university was also building a new $27 million library addition, a new $5 million art museum, and beginning the largest scholarship campaign in the school's history. Not only does Wefald understand the enormous role that football plays in the public perception of a university, but he personally cares about the football program and the youngsters who take part in it.

After Snyder's visit to Manhattan, he realized that circumstances placed the university at a crossroads athletically. This was a unique opportunity. There was no other "worst program in the country."

Iowa head coach Hayden Fry was one of the first to forecast Kansas State's rise when he said, "I think he will do a job much quicker than anyone anticipates in regards to taking Kansas State to respectability." Former KSU assistant coach Larry Kramer has known Snyder since 1974, when he hired Snyder as his offensive coordinator at Austin College. Kramer talked to Snyder right after he decided to accept Kansas State's offer.

Snyder said, "There is a team of five or six people down there who are ready to do it the right way."

Coach Snyder is asked almost daily, "What convinced you to come to Kansas State?" Apparently there wasn't one particular thing. He has summarized his reasons by saying: [It was] *the impact of a lot of people. I was impressed that the individuals I met were good quality people. That meant a lot to me, and that was the first order of business. But it was more than that. It was their genuine interest in developing Kansas State University, not only the Athletic Department or the football program, but all aspects of the university. People like Jon Wefald, Bob Krause and Steve Miller had a very strong impact on me. I had the same reaction to faculty members, boosters and other constituencies. There was a genuine, sincere, and honest commitment to move Kansas State in a better and more positive direction. I think that, as much as anything, impacted my decision.*

I was also very impressed by the "hard core blue collar" K-Staters who were willing to roll up their sleeves and go to work. I appreciated their sense of loyalty. I appreciated it, not because they had suffered, but because they were still there.

Fortunately Snyder took Kansas State at its word, and did not ask for proof that the money existed to fulfill the promises that were made. Kansas State had a rude awakening concerning the program's facilities. Officials knew that they had a poor press box, but they thought everything else was fine.

Vice President Bob Krause played a critical role in this phase of the process. He approached prominent boosters and appealed to them to help Kansas State. Gradually, the university's hard work and commitment began to pay off, but a little luck helped too. The stadium was badly in need of new artificial turf; it was in such poor condition that it was dangerous. Dave Wagner, of Dodge City (class of '69), won the $37 million Kansas Lotto America in 1990. Wagner called Steve Miller and told him that he had just won the lottery. He asked Miller what the program needed. Miller said, "Well, you can buy new turf for us, that's a million bucks." Wagner didn't blink, he just said, "Fine." This was a huge contribution to the progress of the program. The turf had to be replaced at the same time that new money needed to be pumped into the operating budget for salaries, additional support staff, and the recruitment budget. Without Wagner's generosity, something else would have had to be put on hold.

Snyder Demonstrates his Concern for Students

The first thing that Snyder did after accepting the position was to ask Joan Friederich, his new secretary and administrative assistant, to set up a meeting with the seniors who would graduate before his first season. Almost all of these players showed up. Looking back at that meeting, some of the players still get "choked up." It meant the world to them that someone cared about them. As one player noted, "Snyder knew that we had a lot of life in front of us and were going to do a lot of things." Former linebacker and captain Rob Goode said, "It was important to Snyder that we felt good about ourselves when we left Kansas State. We will always appreciate that."

Mark Porter, another graduating senior who was at that meeting, recalls "I knew immediately that he really does care about people. He cares about football players being more than football players. The graduating seniors were not 'his players,' yet he sincerely wanted to see us succeed."

Continuous Improvement

Shortly after the meeting with the graduating seniors, Snyder was quoted in *Sports Illustrated: These kids expect so little of themselves now. They came here hoping for so much, and they have gotten so little. That's bad, because if you don't succeed at what you think is important, then it becomes less important.* During his first year at Kansas State, Snyder said, *the first thing we have to learn is how not to beat ourselves. When we learn how to stop losing, then we have to learn how to win.*

One of the most extraordinary aspects of Coach Snyder's philosophy and the success that flows out of it, is his definition of a goal. For many people a goal is a specific, measurable, end product. For Snyder, a goal is actually the adoption of a process. His goal is to make continuous improvement. His number one priority when he first arrived at Kansas State was attitude development. The notion of continuous improvement can be applied to the individual as well as to the group. Such leadership involves identifying one's beliefs and values and being consistent with them; determining a course for change in the future and articulating it as a vision; and developing oneself and others to the highest levels of potential. Each of these steps represents what many authors have referred to as "transformational leadership."

Snyder never talks about wins or losses. He stresses developing an understanding of how not to give up, and an understanding of how and why to expect wins. Snyder has absolute confidence in himself and in his plan. Somehow he saw what no one else could even dream. He did not say it would come quickly. He said, *it's going to be one step at a time. There are not going to be any shortcuts. I'm not going to promise you we're going to win one, two, five, seven or ten. All I can promise you is we're going to get a little bit better every day. And that's not just in football, but in all aspects of their lives. I have no idea how long it will take. I just know it will get done.*

During his first year at Kansas State, he only had 47 players on scholarship; most other schools had the NCAA limit of 95. *But we took advantage of the Midwestern mentality and work ethic and worked to get better, particularly in terms of the intrinsic things. In time, the players realized that we were getting better and gained a lot in terms of confidence.*

Snyder spends a great deal of time and energy helping his players and staff understand the shared vision for the football program. All of his goals are driven by a very clear set of values — one of which is that everyone's work is important to the success of the program. Therefore, each person understands that his or her work is worthwhile. Whether it is the maintenance crew, the office manager, the trainers, the equipment staff, the walk-on freshman, or the All-American fifth-year senior, each person is aware of how their efforts contribute to the goals of the football program. This is speaking to a very powerful human emotion. Everything that Snyder does increases the self-esteem of those around him; one of the fastest ways to help people feel good about themselves is to help them see how their work contributes to the success of the organization. Coach Snyder does this on a daily basis by clearly articulating how each person in the program is working toward a well-understood and shared goal.

You Are Either Moving Toward your Goals or Away from Them

For Snyder, it is not enough to simply work toward a goal — you must do it the "right way." This means that his players are expected to be good students and good community members as well as good athletes. He makes it absolutely clear to his assistants that they are responsible for monitoring and supporting their students' academic progress. Again, Snyder's leadership philosophy is very compatible with the theory of transformational leadership, which is: visionary, developmental, service-oriented, ethical, stimulating, facilitative, and clear in establishing expectations. For Snyder, the ends do not justify the means. Doing it the "right way" is a wake-up call that all leaders must hear.

During that first season, Kansas State only won one game. Many people skip over that year and talk about the second year, when the team won five games and Coach Snyder was chosen Big Eight Coach of the Year, as the point that the turnaround began. We agree with the observation of former KSU quarterback, and current Overland Park business person, Stan Weber:

> I saw the depths that the program had sunk to. In my first year of broadcasting, the year before Snyder's arrival, there were no wins and one tie. Everything was crumbling or had fallen. It was like there was a hole in the ground. When people talk about the Kansas State football program and its growth, they always talk about one win, then five wins, then seven win teams. But they fail to understand that a losing program does not have to stop at "ground zero." During the five years prior to Snyder's arrival at Kansas State, the team won only three games. When a team goes into most of their games without any hope of winning that is worse than just not winning any games. There can actually be negative numbers. When Snyder got here, the team was below the waterline. What he did in his first season was to take a team from a "minus five to a one." People who start to measure his success from the second year forward fail to recognize how much improvement there was during that first year.

Snyder does not believe that it is possible to stay in one place. You are always either moving toward your goal or away from it. With each year without a win, the team was moving farther and farther away from the goal of winning. Weber remembers when he first realized that something exciting was happening at Kansas State.

> It was September 8, 1989, the night before his first game as coach at Kansas State. It was the "walk through" at Sun Devil stadium. You could see that Snyder was doing things the right way. Prior to this season, when the broadcast team went to the

booth, there was no emotion. Everyone knew, with one hundred percent certainty, that Kansas State was going to lose. No one went to the game thinking we could win. Not broadcasters. Not fans. Not coaches. And not players.

What makes Snyder a great leader was very apparent right away. Although you can only expect people to do the best that they can, you should not be embarrassed to expect them to do their best. But, when a team is not winning any games, it is almost an embarrassment for them to act like they are doing their best. The players begin to think, "What difference does it make, we're going to lose no matter what we do, so why pay attention to the little things?"

When Snyder walked out onto that field before that first game, he had a group of players who had no chance of beating Arizona State University. In fact, they had little chance of winning very many games all year. Yet, it was amazing to watch the team come out onto the field. They took the field like they were the national champions. When they went through warmups, when they went from spot to spot on the field, everything was done with the seriousness you see in the current edition of the team.

In that first game, it was obvious that something had happened. The same people who had not won a game the year before were behaving in a way that demonstrated their increased self respect. The core of his leadership philosophy is: Everybody in this program will try to get better all the time. Everybody involved in the program will work extremely hard. Everybody who works in the program must care, and have a great compassion for young people. Everyone in the program tries every single day to become a better person.

We agree with Bob Krause when he notes, "Leadership is never over. It is a constant journey. You can stop along the way and appreciate what has happened, but leadership continues. There are not limits other than those we place on ourselves or allow others to place upon us." The turnaround of the Kansas State football program is a tangible example of a continuous process of improvement. What Bill Snyder has done at Kansas State can be a model for anyone interested in improving an organization and the people in it.

For further information about transformational leadership we recommend:

Bass, B. M., and Avolio, B. J. (1994). *Improving Organizational Behavior Through Transformational Leadership*. Thousand Oaks, CA: Sage.

Burns, J. M. (1978). *Leadership.* New York: Harper and Row.

Rost, Joseph C. (1991). *Leadership for the Twenty-First Century*. New York: Praeger.

Chapter One

Vision and Goal Attainment

Introduction

$\mathcal{I}$ MPROVING A COMPANY, organization, or football team involves the ability to envision change. Change, however, does not occur in isolation; it occurs within a context. In this chapter, and in those that follow, the success of the Kansas State University football program will be the context that we will use to look at leadership. We will present Coach Snyder's leadership philosophy as a model of how a leader can initiate and nurture the change process. Additionally, we will include comments from a variety of others — players, staff, business leaders, K-State administrators, faculty, and students — who substantiate the success of this model.

Each chapter consists of a number of lessons clustered around a major leadership theme. Chapter One includes five Leadership Lessons that address the issues of vision, value based goal setting, decision making, and goal attainment.

Lesson One outlines Coach Snyder's unique goal attainment process. Readers will find a clearly delineated and easy-to-follow three-step approach.

Lesson Two focuses on the importance of establishing and promoting a vision of change before implementing the goal attainment process.

Lesson Three explains the concept of balancing daily improvement and long-term goals. Snyder believes that to focus only on future goals is counterproductive.

Lesson Four highlights the central theme of Coach Snyder's entire philosophy: daily improvement will eventually bring long-term success.

Lesson Five presents a sensible strategy for efficiently making decisions that are appropriate for each individual.

Leadership Lesson Number One

Goal attainment is a three-step process: a) significant goals are set based on priorities/values; b) a well-constructed plan is put into place; and c) a "just do it" attitude is adopted.

The goal attainment process begins with the identification of priorities that will serve as the basis for goal selection. Values are often referred to as "guiding principles," or those things that give life purpose. Coach Snyder believes that goals should be based on values and be significant and worthwhile. Snyder developed the goals for the football program by merging and synthesizing two sets of values: those that are necessary in any organization, and those that came directly from his assessment of what existed at Kansas State University when he arrived.

Everybody in our program establishes goals on a very regular basis. We establish daily, weekly, and long-range goals. This is not a unique idea; many people establish goals. However, what may be more significant, is that we consciously establish goals that are consistent with our values and are very significant to us! We spend a lot of time with this first step, determining those things that we would like to accomplish that address our priorities. The reason that this is such an important step is so that we do not expend time and energy working toward goals that are insignificant. We establish goals based on our priorities. Then we attempt to make all decisions in relationship to how our actions relate to these goals.

The two most important areas of life are your faith and your family. This is true for student-athletes, students in general, and citizens at large. Beyond these two values, each individual has to determine what is important to him or her. These areas could include career goals, personal development goals, or academic goals. Once our players have addressed the goals related to faith and family, they must next identify the other things that they want to accomplish. It is important to me that our student-athletes establish goals that will allow them to become the best student, the best person, and the best football athletes they can be. We ask them to base their goals on their priorities. Basically, "what would you like to achieve in each one of those particular categories?"

In our program, we have sixteen "Wildcat Goals for Success." We orient all that we do around these goals and reinforce them frequently. The sixteen goals are:

1. Commitment
2. Unselfishness
3. Unity — come together as never before
4. Improve — Every day . . . as a player, person, and student
5. Be Tough
6. Self-discipline — Do it right, don't accept less
7. Great Effort
8. Enthusiasm
9. Eliminate mistakes — Don't beat yourself up
10. Never give up
11. Don't accept losing
12. No Self-limitation — Expect more of yourself
13. Expect to Win
14. Consistency
15. Leadership
16. Responsibility

We start each season by talking about each of these sixteen goals, and then working on each goal on a regular basis. I go into much more depth as to exactly what each goal means and how we should work toward that goal. I am a strong believer in being consistent. We have a good plan and we don't make changes unless there is a demonstrated reason. Our youngsters can relate to consistency. We create a pattern in their daily life, and then they learn to work within that routine. I think you get better at doing something by doing it over and over again.

At first glance this process of establishing goals may seem like "old hat." Setting goals based on priorities is not a new idea. Many people do this. They may write their goals on a piece of paper and refer to them frequently. They may even put them on the mirror in their bathroom. There are a hundred things that may be very meaningful and significant in that process. However, the important thing is for youngsters, or anyone for that matter, to be very honest with their self-assessment, and be very honest when identifying their priorities. The goals must reflect the person's values.

?

How do you motivate players to compete with the intensity necessary to play at the collegiate level?

Tim Taylor
Class of '01, El Dorado, Kansas

Teach players to understand that they control the effort and intensity with which they practice and play. Demand that from them. Stress holding each other and yourself accountable.

Coach Snyder

Max Urick, K-State Director of Athletics, confirms that Coach Snyder is sincerely interested and responsive to the priorities and values of others. "When we first met, we talked about working together and about our goals and values. A common ground was quickly established."

For Coach Snyder, goal-setting is a life activity, not just a football technique. Mordean Taylor-Archer, Associate Provost, is especially impressed that Coach Snyder helps his players establish academic and career goals: "The emphasis that he places on education is really quite impressive." This is substantiated by the fact that KSU was recognized by the College Football Association three times in the 90's as one of the top thirteen schools in the nation for graduating seniors.

Kathy Greene, Director of KSU Educational and Supportive Services and the mother of two former K-State football players, remembers,

He called a meeting of all of the athletes and said, "We are going to work with you, not only on the football field, but in the classroom. We want you to take something away besides being a football player." During the meeting he referred to academics quite a bit. He said, "You are going to get to a point where the light bulb will click on and then the academics are going to be really important to you." He related athletics and academics to his own background. He said that he wasn't always excited about school, but at a certain point the light bulb turned on for him.

This emphasis of the total person is not lost on his players. Laird Veatch played for Coach Snyder between 1990 and 1994, and is currently director of annual giving for the University of Missouri Athletics Department. He recalls,

> Coach wanted more from you than just being an athlete. He wanted you to be the best player you could be, the best student you could be, and the best person you could be. He always encouraged you to try to get better every day. I know that some people think that is some kind of public relations ploy. It is not. Coach Snyder does not lie.
>
> Playing as a freshman in my home town, there was a lot of pressure on me. K-State was pretty low in the linebacker core when I arrived. They kind of shoved me in there right away. The coach let me know that he believed in me and that I could do it. But he also let me know that I was going to be held to the same standards as everyone else.

Perhaps Manhattan business person Dennis Mullin said it best, "Coach Snyder goes beyond trying to make the guy a success in football. He tries to make the guy a success as a person."

Value Based Goal-Setting

A great deal of who I am comes from my mother. The words that best describe her are persistence and hard work. She was a roll up your sleeves, go to work and get it done type of woman. She was persistent about making a living and raising her son. She had great focus on doing what needed to be done to meet her responsibilities as a mother. She was not easily distracted. Some of her ability to focus on what needs to be done has probably carried over with me.

I have learned from a lot of different people. In some ways, I think everybody was my mentor. From some people I learned things that I wouldn't want to do, and that I wouldn't want to incorporate in my way of doing things. And from others I learned things that seem good and productive. The learning process consisted of a series of: "That works, let's do it that way," and "That doesn't seem so good so let's not do it that way."

For Coach Snyder, it is not enough to select significant values and subsequent goals, you must also prioritize them realistically. Although he believes there are no greater fans than K-State Wildcats (*"K-State fans have impacted my staying here as much as anything"),* he thinks that support for the football program should be put in proper perspective. *When we went to the first bowl game, which would have been the Copper Bowl in Tucson, it is not an exaggeration to say that a thousand people told me that the Copper Bowl experience was the greatest single experience of their life. That's crazy. I don't want our program to come before your faith and your family, or your career.*

This concept of value based goal setting evolved as I began to help our players focus on what needed to be done regarding our football program. After setting goals regarding faith and family, we ask that they set goals in the areas that we believe are essential to our program. Each person has to identify and set goals outside of the football setting that are important in their lives. Accordingly, they need to establish priorities along those lines as well. This process helps each student-athlete focus on both his individual needs and the needs of our program.

Development Plan

While the selection of goals is an important part of the process, it is the development of a plan to accomplish the goals that is what usually differentiates those who are successful from those who are not. There are many people who want to be All-State or All-American, or to stop smoking or to lose weight, or to be the best sales person in the company, but many of these people fall short of these goals. They fail, in part, because they do not have a plan.

People are always reminiscing about their New Year's resolutions. We all make resolutions. However, those well-intended resolutions often go by the wayside over a period of time. New Year's resolutions are goals. They are things that, at some point in time, we thought were important. However, quite obviously they often don't meet the criteria for what is really important to us. If they did really relate to our values, we would stick with them a little bit longer.

Setting goals is the easy part. Virtually everybody sets goals. This is not to imply that goal setting is not important. However, if you expect to achieve your goals, you must make a significant time commitment. You must make a commitment that says "I've got to go about this the right way." Guesswork doesn't count for a great deal. Knowledge is the all encompassing guide. It is important to accumulate knowledge through the right sources. The sources are those people who have achieved, or attempted to achieve, those things which have become important to you. If you want to become a doctor, talk to a successful doctor. If you want to be a lawyer, go talk to a successful lawyer. If you want to be an educator, talk to a successful educator.

If you attach yourself to something below the line, that is the direction you're going. If you attach yourself to something above the line, that's the direction you're going. I tell the players "Be around people who want to make your life better." Why would you want to spend time with or be focused on an individual who does not have your best interest at heart, who would not want to make your life better? Of course, this has to do with your principles, values, behavior, and attitudes. If you're around someone who wants to draw you down or is in a position to draw you down, they will definitely succeed. But, if you are around someone who can lift you above where you are, then that will happen too.

The second, and more difficult step, is the establishment of a well-conceived and well-thought-out plan that will allow you to achieve your goals. Being able to identify the steps that will allow you to go from where you are to where you want to go is a critical part of the process. Developing a very specific plan is the most significant factor in order to have a chance at success. Many people never take this second step. Consequently, designing a plan places you in somewhat elite company. However, it is the third step that makes a person unique. The third step is to actually implement the plan. All plans must be action plans. Having a goal and making a plan are not going to ensure that you reach your goal. You must take the final step. You must be willing to put in hard work in order to reach your goals. The old Nike slogan says it best, "Just do it!"

The importance of taking the final step of doing the work was reinforced when we asked Demetric Denmark, former K-State corner back and a player representative for the 1997 season, what he would tell a high school student who was considering playing at Kansas State. He said, "I would tell them that Snyder is a fair guy, but once you get out on the practice field it is all business. It is a family, but on the field you are your own guy. You must stand up to the task. Coach Snyder is going to expect your best and you have to produce."

Coach Snyder's emphasis on a well-thought-out plan allows him to stay focused and not be distracted from his goals. *Many people are not sure what they are working toward. They get up each day and work hard, but don't seem to be getting anywhere. Accordingly, they may become dis-*

couraged and stop working hard. Snyder's approach is to set a goal and then identify the specific steps that need to be accomplished each day to achieve that goal. In this way you have the opportunity to evaluate your progress on a day-by-day basis, and take satisfaction in your daily accomplishments.

Goals Must Be Stated in Clear and Concrete Terms

Our student-athletes write down their individual goals in each area. I talk to each youngster that is going to enter our program before he comes to campus. We talk about establishing goals. I ask him to write down his goals and send them to me. I like them to do that before they get here because that gives me an opportunity to try to help with the process. Once they're here we have an assessment period three times a year in which each individual reviews his goals with his position coach. A coach then assists him in assessing his progress on each of his goals. After evaluating what has taken place as it relates to their goals, each player establishes future goals for a specific period of time.

The football year is not much different from the year for a corporation in that it is divided into certain segments of time. Our program is divided into four segments: a season, an out of season program, spring football program, and the summer program. Each youngster has football-oriented goals that focus on each of those particular segments. Our coaches visit with each player and they jointly determine the individual's strengths and weaknesses. They then identify the specific steps that the player needs to follow in order to accomplish his goals. We do the same thing with each youngster's academic goals. Additionally, the goal attainment plan recognizes that not all goals can have equal priority all the time. We believe that in order for players to reach their goals, it is necessary that there is support available to assist them. Each of these goal areas — faith, family, student, person, and football athlete — is significant in its own right. Although there is an interaction and a tie between each and every one of these categories, each can stand alone.

Goal Setting Should be Collaborative

In order to be successful, organizations must spend a great deal of time setting goals, designing plans, and implementing those plans. This is a continuous process that must take place at all levels of the organization. In the Kansas State football program, all of the coaches have a great deal of responsibility and authority. *The offensive and defensive staffs are constantly involved in an ongoing process of analyzing their personnel and devising their plans. These plans are formulated through dialogue and discussion and then are presented to me. The plans are then modified and fine tuned. We then break these plans down into manageable segments for instruction. Finally we devise a schedule for introducing the plan to our players.*

Staff members and student-athletes often talk, observe, critique, and plan together. Norms of collective responsibility and continuous improvement encourage each member of the program to teach one another how to improve their performance. By involving his staff and his athletes in collaborative goal setting, he reduces staff isolation, uses organizational mechanisms to support cultural changes, shares leadership with others by delegating power, and actively communicates the program's norms and beliefs.

Often when people think of football players, and athletes in general, they think of self-centered and perhaps selfish individuals. This does not seem to be true in the collaborative atmosphere that Coach Snyder fosters. A perfect example of this cooperative attitude can be seen in comments of running back Frank Murphy, that were reported in the *Manhattan Mercury*.

Murphy readily admits that he is relying on those experienced players to help him, and there do not seem to be any tense feelings among the players. When referring to Marlon Charles and Eric Hickson, veteran running backs, Murphy said, "Eric and Marlon teach me as I go, and they understand the feeling of competition. We know it's whoever's the best man, and I think that's a good attitude to have." He said, "I feel it's a team thing. I feel if I work my butt off and do the right things, then I should get a chance to show my skills. . . ."

Collaboration Includes Fostering Staff Development

Staff members' motivation for development is enhanced when they are committed to goals for professional growth. This process is facilitated when they are strongly committed to the organization's mission. Snyder gives his assistant coaches a significant role in solving non-routine problems. Accordingly, the staff has an opportunity to develop to their maximum capacity. The responsibilities that Snyder assigns to his assistants are explicit and ambitious, but not unrealistic.

This collaborative goal setting and communication process can be seen in the meetings Coach Snyder has with his staff before the start of each season. At these meetings, Snyder reestablishes the staff objectives and specifically delegates power to his staff. He clearly communicates that, *we expect these things from our players and therefore should expect them from each other.* For example Snyder expects his staff to: *take nothing for granted, come together as no staff has, work harder than you ever have before, work smart, expect a lot of yourself and each other, and don't accept less than your best.* He also expects his assistants to teach players every day and motivate players every day. He expects his coaches to see to it that their players stay out of trouble, receive the academic support they need to remain academically eligible, and are motivated to improve every day.

We asked Gordon Brown, former defensive back and current police officer with Kansas State's Department of Public Safety, if he thought that Coach Snyder was concerned about the players' actions off the football field. Gordon laughed, and said, "Are you kidding me? That is one of his biggest concerns. He is always talking about how important it is that we handle ourselves and we carry ourselves appropriately, because we have a lot of young kids that look up to us, as athletes. Before we go out and have a good time, he says, 'Make sure you carry yourself in a professional manner.' This is really a big thing for all of the coaches. This is what he means when he says you have to be accountable. Your actions affect others and you are responsible for what you do."

Develop a Strategy to Identify Future Leaders

On our team, those who become leaders are primarily those who are recognized as having accomplished something that other players in this program would like to accomplish. We have a leadership development process. The first stage is the selection of player representatives. These youngsters provide leadership for our program, and serve as a formal bridge between the staff and the total team. Later in the year the team selects players to the honorary position of team captain. We have developed this process so that a fairly large number of players have a chance to demonstrate and practice their leadership strengths over a period of time. This process also ensures that the team has a base of people from which to choose their captains. This process gives the players an opportunity to determine who really has stepped up and provided the leadership that is needed.

The player representative concept is a way of consolidating some of the decision-making process. We make it clear that the player representative should not simply be a youngster who absorbs information. These should be youngsters who the players will go to for guidance, for direction, and for leadership.

Develop a "Just Do It" Attitude

Sean Snyder, All-American punter and Assistant Athletic Director, believes that attitude is key to success. He states, "I don't know that anyone loves what they do more than my dad. In order to be successful you have to have the inner drive to do what is necessary to get the job done."

Jim Epps agrees that Coach Snyder "will never accept that something can't be done. He will immediately look for other options. Have you tried this? Have you tried that? You have to exhaust all of the options that you have thought of plus the new ones that he is going to present to you. He just never gives up."

Although Coach Snyder was always focused, he was not always focused on the "right things." *I have always been able to focus on what I wanted to do. However, as a youngster I was not always focused on the appropriate things. I could focus on whatever was important to me at that particular point in time of my life. Recently, after my mother died, I was going through some family stuff that we had accumulated and I came across a newspaper article about my involvement in the YMCA. One of the things that the YMCA provided for youngsters was a summer camp. My mother couldn't afford to send me. At that time, there were a lot of youngsters that could not afford the camp. The YMCA had a soap selling program that gave youngsters an opportunity to earn the money for camp. I sold more soap than anyone.*

I believe there were two reasons that I was able to accomplish this. First, I was really competitive. And second, I really wanted to go to camp. I learned that if you want something badly enough and you are willing to work hard, you can accomplish your goals. In my high school years I was distracted from education, and my focus went to other things. I was engrossed in athletics, sports of all kinds. Consequently, there were some really significant and important things in my life that weren't as important to me as they should have been. My priorities weren't in order. That's why I can really understand what many young people are going through today. I think all of us, particularly young people, need help in identifying what is important, establishing a plan, and being motivated to work toward their goals.

Clarifying your goals and making a plan are important, but ultimately meaningless unless you are willing to focus on your plan and put in the tremendous effort and hard work necessary for success. Many of our football athletes are able to translate this process into the academic side of their lives. There is a bombardment process within our system. It is an ongoing process, every day. Part of our ongoing process is to frequently repeat what we want to get across. The three-step process of setting a goal, making a plan and then having the courage and commitment to do the work is stressed over and over. When they leave this program they have a viable process for problem solving.

The Relationship between Collective and Individual Goal Setting

In addition to individual goal setting, you need to do collective goal setting. Whether you are dealing with a football program or a business, you have to do this. Collective goal setting is only effective if all individuals buy into the whole enterprise. They are more likely to buy into it if they have their own goal setting process that helps them to achieve success in their individual areas. Then they begin to realize, over a period of time, that larger organization contributes to their individual success. They will be a little bit more appreciative of the collective goal setting process. I don't think there is a great deal of difference in the process between individual and group goal setting.

Counting the wins and losses of Kansas State's football program is only one indicator that Coach Snyder's goal attainment strategy works. Perhaps a more important measure is seen by talking with young men who have left the program and gone on to take their places in the work force. As we talked to these people, they consistently told us that what they learned while playing football at K-State has helped them find reward in their careers and personal lives. Tim Colston learned the value of education from Coach Snyder.

I had no intention of going to college, coming out of high school. When I first got to Kansas State, I thought I was going to play football, do my time, and then leave. He really stresses education. He changed my thinking. If you missed class he really got on you. I left Kansas State without a degree, but he got me back on campus. I only need one more semester to grad-uate and am enrolled in classes this fall.

Brooks Barta, a teacher and high school football coach, reports that,

Consistency is the story about Coach Snyder. He is the same person with the same values, same expectations, and the same steps now as when he first got there. Snyder does an excellent job of helping individuals understand where they are, where they want to be, and what they have to do to get there. And then he does a good job of executing, monitoring, reevaluating, and going back over the things. I try to do the same thing now as a coach. If you pay attention you can take these things into the world of work.

Chris Cobb, sales manager of a clothing company in Texas, looks to the "Sixteen Wildcat Goals for Success" for inspiration on a daily basis.

Coach Snyder expected each person to make a commitment to each of those goals. You may find it hard to believe, but I use these goals every day. I am a straight commission salesman here in Dallas. All of those principles that he taught me, and that impacted my life when I was a football player, still impact my life every day. The two or three principles that are most important to me are self discipline, responsibility, and to expect to win no matter how difficult the cause or battle. He gave each of us the confidence to expect great things of ourselves. He taught us to never sell ourselves short. He taught us that if we lose, not to accept it, but to understand it. He taught us to give great effort, be enthusiastic, and do not set limits on yourself. In straight commission sales I have to motivate myself if I don't want to let myself or family down.

Matt Miller, former quarterback and current graduate assistant, said it well: "You can talk to anyone — even those who didn't play — and they will say that they left the football program a better person; that Coach was true to his values, and helped each of us be true to ours."

Leadership Lesson Number Two

A vision of the desired transformation must be established before implementing the goal attainment process.

One of the most important aspects of leadership is the ability to provide a clear vision that allows others to understand the transformation, or future, that the leader imagines for the organization, team, or business. Coach Snyder's concept of vision is evident and substantiated by the observations and comments of others.

During the interview process, Snyder impressed the search committee with his articulate, detailed, and thoughtful image of where the K-State football should be headed. Bob Snell, KSU professor and faculty representative to the Big 12 Conference and the NCAA, remembers, "When we asked the other finalists what they would do if they were hired, most said that they would work hard. Snyder was much more specific. It was clear that he had a plan."

Kathy Greene, academic counselor for the football team during Snyder's first year, verifies Coach Snyder's consistent vision for the program.

> He had a vision of where he wanted the football team to be. I think it was his vision that most excited everybody. From the first day that he arrived on campus, he was talking about academic recognition for the players, an academic center for all athletes, and many other things that we had not even thought of.

Coach Snyder demonstrates by his actions that along with establishing a vision you must have determination and the courage of your convictions. The more ambitious the vision, the more important it is to be able to articulate it in a way that most people can easily understand.

Former player and current college football coach Kitt Rawlings often tells his friends and family his favorite story about how he decided to go to KSU.

I was from out west and was being recruited by the WAC schools. I went on several recruiting trips and the various coaches told me what they hoped to do, and what they wanted to see happening in their program. As I was preparing to end my recruiting visit to KSU, Coach Snyder sat me down and said, "Kitt, I would like you to come to Kansas State. I know you have read the Sports Illustrated article, and have heard others talk about us as being 'Futility U.' Let me tell you what we are going to do at Kansas State University." He did not tell me what he wanted to do, or hoped to do, or planned to do. He told me what KSU was going to do. He described the specific improvements that he was going to bring about in the facilities, weight room, etc. He invited me to be part of that.

I love telling that story because, to me, it means so much when you think about your goals. As a result of playing for Coach Snyder, I constantly ask myself and others, "Is this something that you hope to do, or is this something that you are going to do?" I have learned that you need to be decisive and forge forward with things you want to do.

Having a very clear vision of where you want to go has had a significant, positive impact on Laird Veatch's personal and professional life. The constant repetition of the winning expectation was established early and it has been maintained. Veatch remembers that Coach Snyder was always stressing

> . . . that "no self-limitation thing." The year before I got there, Kansas State won one game. Clearly, the biggest obstacle we had to overcome was the negative attitude that had permeated the program. Coach Snyder immediately set about the process of raising all of our expectations. He made us believe we could win any game, and overcome any obstacle. He constantly raises expectations and pushes people to excel. It became second nature to expect to win and to never give up.

Coach Snyder's players quickly developed the "we expect to win" mentality. However, it took a little longer for people outside the football program to understand. Chris Cobb notes that, "When we beat North Texas State, my junior year, the fans tore down the goal posts. Coach was disappointed because the fans showed the team that they thought it was unusual and unexpected that we won. He wanted winning to be so expected that tearing down the goal posts would be ludicrous."

Air Force Major and ROTC instructor Steve Dorfman gives Coach Snyder credit for not only establishing a vision, but for wisely making it a vision that all embrace. According to Dorfman, "A good leader is able to take a vision and get the people to buy into it. It's not really the leader's vision, it's everybody's vision."

> How do you get all of your players to share the same goal?
> Jeremy Hogaboom
> Class of '01, Manhattan, Kansas
>
> *One would think this would be an easy task, since virtually everyone involved in athletics believes that winning is the ultimate goal and they all want to win. The real task is getting young people to realize that there are objectives that must be focused on and achieved before winning the right way can take place. Our emphasis is constantly on those "objectives" which create success and being able to portray countless examples of how successful goals are achieved through a commitment to such objectives as self-discipline, unity, teamwork, responsibility, improvement, unselfishness, accountability, hard work, persistence, perseverance, etc.*
>
> *Coach Snyder*

Long-time observers of Coach Snyder and the football program agree that Snyder is an expert at getting people to share his vision. Michael Holen, Dean of the College of Education, is impressed that "He gets the players to make the team's vision their own. By helping them take the long approach of getting better every day, he teaches them the important lesson that real progress comes incrementally." This is a concept that is essential for leadership in the business world.

Dennis Mullin believes, "A leader is someone who can, not only form a vision, but instill that vision in the people in the organization. Coach Snyder really has that talent." This is the essence of true motivation, to help people care enough about something that they are willing to do the hard work necessary to obtain their goal.

Perhaps the best example of both the difficulty and the impact of helping others to grasp a vision can be seen in the comments of Chris Cobb.

I remember something that happened during Coach Snyder's first summer practice. Some of the players stood up in a players' meeting and said, "What are we going to do about this new coach?" I said, "We are not going to do anything. This team went 0-11. Do we really think we are too cool to follow the rules that Coach wants?" Some of the players wanted to wear earrings and hats. I said, "Hell, we can go 0-11 from here until the sun don't shine, or we can make some changes and win some football games." There were a lot of people who quit that first summer. A ton of people transferred, thinking that they were too good for the coach's ideas. That is one of the reasons that the guys who stuck around are so proud of what we accomplished. Winning five games in a year made us all feel like we won eleven games. As we seniors prepared to leave the program, we knew that we were going to miss something very special, and sure enough we have. I dream about it all the time, and wish I could go back and be part of today's team.

Leadership Lesson Number Three

Goal attainment is always a balance between focus on long-range goals and daily improvement.

One aspect of Coach Snyder's leadership philosophy that is unique is his ability to teach the concept of simultaneously holding a short- and long-range goal. This concept is central to his goal attainment process.

People who talk about goal setting often say, "Keep your eye on your goal." They imply that if you keep your eye on the goal you will have a better chance of achieving it than if you lose sight of your goal. It is important not to misinterpret this statement. To my way of thinking, you need to pay attention to the plan, and the steps that are necessary to achieve your goal. If I spend too much time with my eye on the goal, I'm not going to be able to focus on taking the right steps, and therefore I won't achieve my goal. Many people know where they are, and where they want to end up, but they have no idea how to get there. They work very hard and sometimes end up far from where they started, but no nearer to their goal. They may have kept their eye on the goal all along, but they didn't get any closer because they did not have a plan. Or if they had a plan they did not follow it.

How small should you make the incremental steps of an improvement plan?

Lindsay S. Weir
Class of '98, Manhattan, Kansas

Small enough to avoid taking any short cuts. The steps (objectives) should be detailed enough that you are continually building a strong foundation. No detail is too small if it can be seen as a viable part of the big picture.

Coach Snyder

The ability to have a long-range goal, while at the same time keeping an eye on the incremental steps of your plan, is a lesson that has been learned well by Snyder's former players. Mike "Crash" Ekeler, director of sales and marketing for a Nebraska firm, remembers how incredible it was to watch Snyder build a program from the ground floor. Mike and his father were recently commenting that Coach Snyder is an inspiration to them in their company. Mike reports that he uses what he learned from Snyder on a daily basis.

I have learned how to pay attention to the little things. It does make a difference. Coach has a saying, "You have to trade in one day of your life for what you do that day, and you have to make it worth it." Everyday when I get up and come to work, I want to outwork everybody who works here, and everybody that works at every other company in my industry.

Leadership Lesson Number Four

The ultimate goal of leadership is continuous improvement, rather than a quantifiable outcome.

Rather than focusing on achieving quantifiable goals, such as "so many wins" or "so many sales" or "such-and-such grade point average," Coach Snyder consistently encourages people to focus on becoming the best student, employee, parent, or athlete that we can conceivably be.

Striving to accomplish a goal requires discipline. Often there is a lack of immediate gratification. Clearly, quantifiable goals are much easier to conceptualize than is the goal of continuous improvement. Yet it is necessary to be able to sense progress toward your goal in order to be willing to continue to strive for it. Coach Snyder believes that the ultimate goal of being as successful as one can possibly be is not in conflict with the ability to appreciate short term goals such as winning a game or receiving individual recognition.

Breaking the Goal Down into Manageable Pieces

It's a little different in terms of how we succeed as a football team as opposed to how you succeed in your own personal life or career. Although the process is fundamentally the same, it might not structurally be exactly the same. As far as our football program, I don't really see a conflict with what we might term a short-term daily goal, and a long-term goal. For us, the long-term goals are basically ongoing. However, the player's ultimate goal and mine are not always the same. He may have a greater fix on a goal such as winning so many games or winning a championship than I do. My goals are ... "let's be as successful as we conceivably can be, let's find a way to improve daily as a person, as a student, and as a football athlete."

Therefore, there is always the goal of improvement. The specific areas of improvement are unique to each individual. However, each individual shares the collective goal of team improvement. Our process is to focus on daily improvement. Every day we want to take those areas that are prior-

ities to us, and find that way in which we can become better. Which, in my way of thinking, is a pretty simple process. Staying on task might be a little difficult, but all of us can find a way to become better at some area of our lives. That's not hard. The hard part is to continue to work over a period of time, but that is habit-forming as well. Once we create those positive habits, we can stay with them on a regular basis. Consequently, if we keep focused on the steps necessary to get better, we will get better.

We then expand this idea of continuous improvement into a team concept. If we have one hundred twenty youngsters getting better, then collectively we become one hundred twenty-fold better than we were at the outset. If we can do that on a regular basis, what's the ultimate? Where does it stop? It stops when we cease to be a collective unit. It stops when you leave this program. It remains for those who are here. It is a matter of trying to get youngsters to buy into that; not only does it benefit them, it benefits the program and the team effort. This relates to establishing a plan, because obviously the plan says that you have to get better in order to get to step A, and get a little better to get to step B, etc. A goal such as "I want to get better" is too general. Goals must be broken down into specific steps. This process helps each football athlete incorporate their individual goals under the umbrella of the team goals. These steps may be so small that they are hard to see on a day-by-day basis, but over time progress shows. When I can reach the second rung of the ladder by getting better, I gain confidence that I can reach the third rung of the ladder, etc.

Athletes learn fair play, teamwork, self reliance, resilience, and competition; this is probably true in any program. The unique thing about Coach Snyder is that he has consciously developed a specific plan that incorporates value lessons. He talks about honesty and integrity and expects to see them demonstrated by his staff and student-athletes. As they establish goals in the area of football, they are also establishing goals as young men. He helps them break their goals down into incremental pieces that are so small that everybody, every day, can ask themselves, "Am I moving toward my goal or away from my goal? Is what I am doing making me better or making me worse?" The people in his program do not have to get from page one to page one thousand; they only have to get one paragraph done each day. They have a plan that will tell them what they have to do to get that one paragraph done. The students that go through Coach Snyder's program learn that if you stick to the plan you do have success. Michael Smith, assistant coach and former player, captured the essence of

Snyder's plan when he said, "If you improve each day as a student, and as an athlete, and as a person, ultimately you are going to be a pretty well-rounded individual."

Deb Patterson, women's basketball coach, observed that with Coach Snyder "You get a feeling that there's a constant process of work and improvement going on, that it's not just about the destination. It's almost as though the destination is secondary to the journey." Bob Krause observed, "The lessons Coach Snyder teaches his players — preparation, commitment, dedication — are lessons that are needed for any organization to succeed."

Help People Focus on Their Progress

Early in the program, we understood that team successes may be few and far between in terms of the final outcome of a game. The important thing was that we needed to establish those particular, small ongoing goals that needed to be achieved, where we could show improvement. In other words, somebody had to be able to sit down and say "OK, yes I did, I did get better today. I did have success, and here is how the success was measured." So we had to be able to measure, not by the outcome of Saturday afternoon, but certain things that you did at practice. We identified ways in which a youngster himself could improve his performance on each task we asked him to perform. We had to closely monitor each individual in order to be in a position to evaluate individual progress. This was the only way that he could see, on a regular basis, that he was getting better.

How far down the road should you set your long-range goal? Would you suggest making a three-year plan or a five-year plan?
Aaron Otto
Class of '98, Manhattan, Kansas

We don't establish goals to meet a time frame. If we improve on a steady basis we will normally achieve the ultimate goals we have set based on the degree of improvement. We have never had a three-year or a five-year plan.

Coach Snyder

During that first season, I would go into the locker room every day, every single day after practice, and talk with virtually every single young- ster and ask each one exactly the same question, "Did you get better today?" The answer eventually became "yes," because they just didn't want to say no. Then I asked them to identify for me where they got better. Pretty soon everyone came to understand the concept of continually work- ing toward improvement. I think this is a very important concept.

During a nearly three-hour practice, they were being asked to do a lot of different things. Athletics, just as any endeavor or career, encompasses many different activities and competencies that are fundamental to suc- cess. Maybe each player didn't get better at every activity, and in all likelihood didn't, but I wanted each player to be able to see progress. I wanted them to understand that you may come off the field feeling as though you had a miserable practice, or you may come home from work thinking you had a miserable day at work. But, wasn't there something where you really did make some headway and you got better? On the practice field, you may have become a better tackler, a better blocker. Maybe some other areas of the game weren't better than they were the day before, but each player could see improvement. By getting better each day at different activities, then pretty soon each category was improving. And collectively, over a period of time, the team got better. This is the process we use to ensure continuous progress, both individually and as a team.

Coach Snyder not only expects each player to improve every day, he also expects his assistant coaches to take every opportunity to improve. He reminds them not to waste a moment. *We will have approximately one hundred and twenty players in our program. Every minute that the players are preparing for the season equals two hours of team improvement.*

Goal Setting Translates to Career and Personal Decision Making

All of the players that we talked with reported that they try to keep in touch with their coaches, often calling or stopping by when they are in Manhattan. It is clear that the football program is sincerely interested in how former players do after they leave the program. This concern is not only shared by the coaching staff, but by the other support staff as well. The most vivid example of this came one day when we asked Joan Friederich, Coach Snyder's secretary and administrative assistant, for help in contacting some of the players who were at Kansas State during Coach

Snyder's early years. We were amazed that she not only knew where the players were, but who recently received a promotion, got married, or had a baby. It is clear that the players in this program are much more than numbers.

Business leaders comment that many younger employees have poor work habits, and take quite a bit of time to adjust to the workplace. Others speak of how young people do not have very much pride in their work or loyalty to their company. It seems to us that loyalty is a two-way street. Our conversations with former players indicate that if the people leading the organization demonstrate that they value the people in the organization, there will be a commensurate loyalty in return.

However, this transition does not take place overnight. Younger players entering the football program need to relearn a lot of behaviors. Coach Snyder reflects, *this program expects a great deal from each youngster. Sometimes youngsters find it difficult to buy into the program because much of what we do is in conflict with what they may have come to believe is acceptable behavior. We continually hammer home the process of making a commitment and working hard over a period of time. It is ingrained enough that they come to understand what we are doing. Many of our former players tell me that at sometime during their tenure here, or after they have finished their tenure, they experience a feeling of, "Wow — I get it!"*

A youngster who is now in medical school came back to visit with me a few days ago. He said that every single day of his life he is motivated by the concept of getting better each day. I don't know if he is going to be successful or not, but the point is that he has a process, by which he attempts to achieve success. That is the key element in all that we do here, that you have a process about how you do things. Without a process you may try this for a while, then try that for a while, then something else. Any success that you have is "hit and miss." I think this lack of a plan and a clear process is a major problem with society today. People just bounce around from one thing to another. Sometimes they hit on something positive, but more often than not they don't. Thus many people find that their results are every bit as scattered as their attempt to get there.

Mike "Crash" Ekeler is a good example of what Coach Snyder is talking about. He recounts that Coach Snyder "helped us understand the big picture. Sometimes you get so tied up on your individual assignments that you forget how what you do fits into what everyone else does."

Leadership Lesson Number Five

Decision making is: a) conscious and based on established values and priorities; b) participatory within well-defined limits; and c) occasionally intuitive.

Decision making and a focus on value-based goals are inseparable for Coach Snyder. He and his staff ask the players to take five or ten seconds each time they are faced with a decision, and ask themselves: *"Does this decision move me toward my goals or away from them? Does it make me a better person? Will it make me a better student? Will it make me a better football athlete?" If the answer is "Yes," then go for it and go for it with great enthusiasm. If the answer is "No" to any of those questions, then there's a pretty good reason to back away. It takes a lot more courage to walk away from some situations than it does to interact.*

Of course, there are some "big" decisions that everyone recognizes are important at the time. But, often seemingly insignificant decisions may be just as important. Everyone has decisions to make every day, with the outcome of any one decision possibly having an impact on the rest of his or her life. Some will have minimum impact, some only have a moderate impact, but some will have a dramatic impact. Because you often don't know which of these decisions will have a dramatic impact on your life, you must take all decisions seriously.

Just as one small decision can negatively affect your life, positive change will come only if you can string together a long series of small, positive decisions. This is not an abstract theory for Coach Snyder. He takes every opportunity to help his players understand how this process works in their lives. Business person and former player Kirby Hocutt's fondest memory of Coach Snyder relates to an event that occurred during his freshman year. Although Kirby doubts that Coach Snyder remembers the incident, it made a very big impression on him:

It was my redshirt freshman year, which a lot of times can be the longest year of your life because you are not getting to play on Saturdays. Somehow, Coach Snyder learned that I was spending too much time in Aggieville.

One night, as I was leaving study hall, Coach motioned me to come over. He put his arm around me and we walked into his office. We just stood there, and he still had his arm around me. He said, "Kirby, I understand you have been spending quite a bit of time in Aggieville." I said, "Well, yes sir, I do like to have a good time now and then." He smiled and said he would like to ask me a couple of questions. "First, is spending time in Aggieville going to make you a better person?" I said, "No sir." He then asked, "Well is spending time in Aggieville going to make you a better student?" And I said, "No sir." He then asked, "Will spending time in Aggieville make you a better football player?" And I said, "No sir." He stood there for a minute and said, "Why don't we cut that back then?" I definitely cut my time in Aggieville back. He made me realize the commitment that was going to be required of me at Kansas State in order to accomplish the goals and objectives that I had set for myself.

Players are constantly given the opportunity to practice decision making. John Butler, funeral director and former player, believes that

Players are making decisions all the time. On every single play each player may have to make fifteen or twenty different decisions on what to do. We practice so much that those decisions on the field become just about routine so you do not panic. But it takes time to learn the system. You make decisions every day in business and you just get used to it. You make better decisions if you have thought about alternatives before they arise.

Role of Participation in Decision Making

When we asked Coach Snyder about the role of participation in decision making, he responded, *I think we incorporate a method of allowing individuals to flourish within the system. Any system that you have has to have some boundaries. Beyond those boundaries the system cannot succeed. If the system can't succeed, then the mutual goals are not going to be achieved. Athletics is only one of those environments — the business world is one of those environments as well. In our program, we don't want to diminish the ability of any youngster to flourish in his own right, but it has to be within a system. For example, if you can run a hundred yards with a football, and cross the goal line without being touched, but you chose to do it going the opposite direction, then your individuality has flourished. However, you have also allowed the structure to collapse and you have not reached the team's goals. I am not supportive of a system that would say "Here's the ball, go play the game."*

There is a lot of room for innovation and creativity in our system, but it must take place within the system. There may be other circumstances and organizations that are more conducive to a greater amount of democracy. I think that one of the functions of leadership is to provide guidance. Most people want guidance and direction. Few of us want to stand out there on a broken limb with no one helping hold the limb up. We all like challenges, but we also all need help in that respect. Players and coaches in our program are put into positions to make decisions. I want our players to make some of the decisions that have significance and importance to them. The important thing is to ensure that they understand that allowing them to make the decisions requires that they live with the consequences as well.

For example, our players make the decisions in regard to what their training rules are. I know what I would prefer to do and what I would like to do, and I do obviously place some restrictions on them; a lot of restrictions in some cases. There is not much that we do where I don't ask for input from our players. They know that it will be input that I will abide by and make decisions according to their wishes, or they will understand that it will be input that I will absorb and make my decisions with their input well considered. They always know on the front end whether this will be their decision as a team, or whether it will be my decision with their input. That's exactly the same way that I work with our coaching staff.

Former players agree that they had many opportunities to make decisions and their input was heard and respected by Coach Snyder. Quentin Neujahr, of the Jacksonville Jaguars, vividly recalls one incident where the team and the coaches had a different point of view. It occurred late in one of Coach Snyder's first seasons.

Coach Snyder was really making us work hard. The guys came to me, as team captain, and said "You got to talk to the coach. We are beat up. We are not going to make it unless we get a break." I remember walking up the stairs of the locker room. I walked into his office and I said, "Hey Coach, the guys downstairs are beat up, and they are hurting." He said, "OK, I will take it under advisement." That is all he said. I told the guys that the coach knew the situation and we will see what he does. He allowed us to go without pads for a practice. Although the other coaches believed that we needed the contact to get better, he responded to our request. That is just one example of the players being involved in joint decision making. It meant a great deal to us to know that our thoughts were valued.

Kevin Lockett, of the Kansas City Chiefs, recalls that Coach Snyder gave each player as much responsibility as the player could handle.

During my senior year, the coach put a lot of pressure on me, not only to perform well and help lead the offense, but to help the other guys who had not played. He challenged me to learn not only my position, but a lot of the other positions. He wanted me to understand what the other guys on offense were doing. I think this was really helpful. There were several instances where there was so much going on in the game that Coach Snyder had to depend on his players to give him good information. There were times when he and I would talk one-on-one on the sideline and we would make decisions together. I would have a lot of input into the decisions.

Matt Garber, assistant high school principal, has to make tough decisions every day. He recalls, "As a quarterback, decision making is a very important process. Coach Snyder explains that preparation builds confidence. Often you do not have the time to think too much. I certainly find that true on my current job. Sometimes you have to act."

Of course, football is not life and life is not football. However, many of Snyder's insights transfer directly to the world of work. For example, most successful businesses have expended a huge amount of effort developing their plans. Those that have no plan will only be able to react to the initiatives of others. However, Coach Snyder has demonstrated that having a well-thought-out plan does not prevent him from making decisions that seem to go against the plan. Organizations that are extremely structured do not have the flexibility to adapt to changing conditions.

Going the Next Step — Delegating Responsibility to Subordinates

Our coaches have the responsibility to provide different directions. I'm open to changing directions, but I am hard in this respect. You can't just throw something out to me and expect me to buy into it. . . . Maybe being born in Missouri happens to have something to do with it, but I want you to be able to prove to me that your idea is better than what we currently do. The reason I want you to prove this to me is because I want you to have a well-thought-out plan. I want you to have all your ducks in order, and I want you to have really put some thought into your suggestion. The easy thing in athletics, or anything else, is to see what someone else does. You see that this business operates this way; they market this way, they package their product this way. It is the same in football — this team does this thing with their offense, and this team does this thing with their defense. It's easy to pay attention to this because it's different. Sometimes it is only because it's different that there is a heightened enthusiasm for it. If you are interested in change, you must be able to support it with appropriate data, have a well organized plan, and be enthusiastic. I'm not one to let boredom set in. What we do is not too boring, I can assure you of that.

Snyder is a leader who stimulates his staff members to engage in new activities and put forth that extra effort. He helps them work harder and smarter. He genuinely believes that his assistant coaches can develop better solutions than he could alone. He demonstrates this belief in the way that he delegates responsibility to his staff. He expects them to be precisely organized. Whether it be in leading drills, teaching skills, conducting meetings, allocation of resources, or interacting with players, Snyder expects his staff to finish what they schedule. He expects each assistant coach to have a daily plan to keep the players motivated and enthused. Dedication and persistence are key concepts for Snyder. He expects his staff to devote all of their activities to the goal of helping the other coaches and players improve.

Snyder works directly with each player, however, he gives his assistants a great deal of responsibility for their players. Although he is kept informed about the progress of each of his athletes, he expects his assistants to handle most problems. He asks each assistant to hold his fellow assis-

tants accountable to each other. The K-State coaching staff expects a lot
from the players and from each other.

Snyder demands discipline, and he expects that activities on and off the
field be done correctly. He frequently holds conversations about "What it
takes to improve," and fosters a positive problem-solving atmosphere by
discouraging negative comments and complaining. Each of his coaches
must have a plan for recruiting, preparation for opponents, administrative
responsibilities, and monitoring player progress. He gives his staff great
freedom, but he expects them to take advantage of it and not abuse it. Snyder makes it clear to all of his staff that, *the most important and valuable
achievement you can contribute to the success of the season is living up to
the team expectations.*

?

Why do you think so many people make decisions that seem to go
against their values?

Maggie Keating
Class of '98, Marysville, Kansas

*Perhaps because they do not have a process by which they make all
of the decisions, a process based upon their priorities and what is
really important to them (i.e., If I do this, will it make me a better parent or teacher, or contractor, etc.). Self discipline may also be a factor.*

Coach Snyder

Strategies for Solving Problems More Effectively

Some specific examples of strategies that Snyder uses to accomplish his
goals are:

- Visits each day with virtually every student-athlete and coach.

- Involves his whole staff and team in deliberating team goals,
  beliefs, and visions at the beginning of each year.

- Helps his players and coaches work smarter by actively seek-
  ing different interpretations and checking out assumptions.
  Individual problems are viewed from the larger perspective of
  the team.

- Avoids commitment to preconceived solutions; he clarifies and summarizes key points during meetings; and keeps the group on task.

- Gives everyone responsibilities and involves staff in significant decision making.

- Finds the good things that are happening and publicly recognizes the work of staff and student-athletes who have contributed to the continued improvement of the team.

- He is receptive to student-athletes' attitudes and ideas. Uses active listening and shows people he truly cares about them.

- Has high expectations for staff and student-athletes. He makes it absolutely clear that he wants his them to be the best they possibly can be.

- Uses organizational mechanisms to support the program, such as finding money to improve the facility and increase the salaries for his assistant coaches.

- Protects his student-athletes and staff from problems created by distractions.

Although some of his methods have been criticized in the media, they can be easily understood if they are seen in light of the overall goal of helping his players become better each day. He is convinced that improvement requires focus and that focus can be damaged as the result of outside distractions. For example, one of the first changes Snyder made upon arriving at Kansas State University was to close all practices. This decision is understandable if seen from the point of view of a coach attempting to maximize every opportunity to help his staff and players improve. Snyder has noted that, *Eighteen-year-old players are easily distracted even without people walking around the field or watching them from the sidelines. The addition of these distractions draws their attention from the task at hand and will not help the players or the team improve.*

Role of Intuition

In football, as in all aspects of life, we can do all the planning we want, but there will be certain things that take place in the course of an event or ball game that are not accounted for. It is important to remember that all the while we are doing our preparation, our opponents are also preparing for the game. For example, we scout ourselves, look for our own tendencies, and modify our approach as a result of this self-assessment. However, football is not an exact science. The event you are planning for will never take place exactly like you would hope. Much of what happens is spontaneous. Consequently, there has to be some flexibility. If you are inflexible and your plan is all cut and dried, you will likely not have the outcome you desire. We have all seen examples of people who follow their plan until they step off the cliff.

Intuition has a part to play in decision making. However, intuition is different than sitting on the floor and making decisions off the seat of your britches. Making decisions on a whim — "let's try this!" — sometimes works, but I think it fails more often. Our concept of intuition is based on many years of experience. It is really a type of probability analysis. I've been involved in coaching for thirty-five years, and over that period of time you find yourself in many, many situations.

One of the most interesting things about football is there are so many variables. You've got eleven guys and the other team has eleven guys, and every thirty seconds they all are going to do something. And believe me, all twenty-two guys never do exactly what it was diagrammed for them to do. There are no plays in football that work just exactly like we put them up on the board. It just doesn't happen that way. There are these different variables and as soon as one variable changes it changes everything in the entire equation. There are a countless number of things that contribute to the outcome every time the ball is snapped.

You may go five years without seeing a similar set of circumstances and then suddenly there it is again. There is something about people who succeed in this profession that allows them to remember and recall specific events from the past. I may not be able to remember very much about a particular ball game five, ten, or fifteen years later, but I will see something happen on the field, and I will immediately say, "Iowa versus Indiana in 1984 — same situation." Experience guides me in making decisions that are very spontaneous.

We want our players to be so well prepared that they can do the same thing in a game situation. The essence of our offensive system is to provide our players, particularly our quarterback, with the ability to make decisions. We believe that the players on the field are in the best position, with the best vantage point to make critical decisions. The ideal situation is to have your team so well prepared that each time the defense presents itself we will know exactly what we need to do. We coaches in the coaching box and on the sideline see the defense and may know what we would like to do in a given situation, but there is not enough time for us to get that information to the players on the field. It is the player on the field that must make adjustments. Then, the defense may make another adjustment and you must counter, if you have the time. This is true with a lot of things that we do on both sides of the ball. The very best players get to the point where they can make a spontaneous decision based on their experience and training.

Michael Smith, All-American receiver and running back coach, puts the decision-making process into perspective when he says,

> In order to be successful, the players and the coaches must be prepared. If we have paid attention to details during practice, and go out on Saturday knowing what we are doing, that is when confidence takes over. When we coaches know our game plan inside and out, we are then ready for any situation. That is the way we prepare, and that is the way we coach our players to prepare themselves. Therefore, when a player comes to the sideline and says, "They are doing this or that," we are all on the same page. We all know what we have to do to stop it or to attack it.

The amount of communication that takes place on the field may not be apparent to the people who watch a ball game from the stands. If you were to be in the stadium when fans are not in the stands and the only noise was the sound that came from the field, you would be amazed at the amount of communication that takes place among the players. It is not just the quarterback, linemen are constantly talking to each other, communicating certain things that are happening and then changing their assignments. All of the players have the responsibility to make adjustments. That's true on both sides of the ball. There is a flexibility in the system that allows those who do the work to make the decisions. Obviously, there is a great deal of instruction and guidance that goes into helping each player at each position understand what those decisions are, and when certain choices need to be made.

Former linebacker Laird Veatch recalls a vivid example of a decision that was based on established values and priorities, including significant participation, and incorporated intuition:

> Coach Snyder never missed a beat. It seemed almost magical the way he anticipated almost everything that could happen. I remember one practice where Coach Snyder and Coach Levitt, the defensive coordinator at the time, came up with a new signal. The signal was only to be used if the coaches wanted the defense to call a time out two, three, or four plays down the road.
>
> Generally this does not take place. Usually if a coach wants a time out he will just signal that he wants one and we call it. When we got this new signal, the players thought we were never going to use it. But then, just three games later, a situation arose where we needed the new signal. It was the last couple minutes of the half, the clock was running, and the coaches did not have a chance to call a time out because the other team was running their two minute offense. One of the coaches gave us the signal, and a couple of plays later we were able to call the time out. There was a very strong wind. Being able to call the time out allowed us to get the ball with the wind at our backs. That one call made a real difference in the outcome of the game. To this day, it is amazing to me that that thought even came to his mind. He is always finding the angle and taking the extra step that most people don't even see.

Theoretical Context

Max DePree, in *Leadership is an Art*, states that "Vision is the basis for the best kind of leadership. Instinctively, most of us follow a leader who has a real vision and who can transform that vision into a meaningful and hopeful strategy. People with a vision . . . embark on voyages to new worlds." Coach Snyder's development of the vision of continuous improvement is clearly different from what many people think of as a goal. He does not focus his attention on the final product. His vision is to have a program that gets better every day. This is a world view that is new for both football in general, and Kansas State football in particular.

Even more importantly, this goal of continuous improvement is compatible with practicing leadership with a purpose. Coach Snyder believes that the ultimate purpose of football is to develop and transform players into better students, athletes, and people. Far too often, leadership books focus on the "how" rather than the "why" of leadership. Coach Snyder's leadership is grounded in solid values and a sincere belief in promoting the "common good."

For further information about vision and goal attainment we recommend:

Bass, B.M. (1990). "From Transactional to Transformational Leadership: Learning to Share the Vision." *Organizational Dynamics*, 18(3).

Covey, S.R. (1991). *Principle-Centered Leadership*. New York: Summit Books.

DePree, M. (1989). *Leadership is an Art*. New York: Doubleday.

Nanus, B. (1992). *Visionary Leadership: Creating a Compelling Sense of Direction for your Organization*. San Francisco: Jossey-Bass.

Wheatley, M. (1994). *Leadership and the New Science: Learning About Organization from an Orderly Universe*. San Francisco: Berrett-Koehler.

Chapter Two

Equality,
Diversity,
and Ethics

O N THIS CHAPTER we examine the application of equality, diversity, and ethics in value-based leadership. Coach Snyder challenges us all to "commit ourselves to moral leadership." This chapter includes four Leadership Lessons that address the issues of respect, diversity, anti-discrimination, and service, and delineate the "what" and "how" of moral leadership.

Lesson Six focuses on balancing equal treatment and respect for individual differences.

Lesson Seven outlines a process for successful diversity education.

Lesson Eight discusses the concept of zero tolerance for discriminatory attitudes or actions as a part of ethical leadership.

Lesson Nine explores the connection between service to others and loyalty to group members.

Leadership Lesson Number Six

Treating everyone equally while respecting individual differences, needs, and motivations is the key to fairness.

Understanding and appreciating individual differences while treating each person fairly is at the heart of coaching. It is axiomatic that everyone in our program will be treated equally by the coaches and by the other players. For me, it's just an easy thing to say — there's no black, there's no white, there's no poor, there's no rich, there's no super-intelligent, and there are no dullards. My players are not faceless by any stretch of the imagination. Each player has his own personality. Individual personalities is what coaching is all about. I think how we treat each individual is directly transferable to the workplace. Everyone is unique and everyone should be treated fairly.

It is evident that his philosophy is understood and appreciated by his players. According to Quentin Neujahr,

> The clearest indication of Coach Snyder's ethical standards is that he treats everyone the same. He expects everyone to be a good student. If a student was having trouble in the classroom, Coach went out of his way to make sure that that student had access to every available resource to help him succeed. If the student decided not to make the effort to succeed in the classroom, there were consequences. One of the things Coach Snyder would do was to hold early morning workouts for those who were not being responsible to their studies. He would make you get up early and run. He would not care who you were. He wanted to see everyone succeed and everybody graduate. That was a very big thing for him. He would see that you spent extra hours in study hall. If you needed a tutor, he would see that academic advisors set up a tutor for you. If he knew that you could be a better student he helped you become better.

Demetric Denmark told us that,

> Coach Snyder is a real sympathetic guy. He really tries to bring back guys who have left without graduating. He keeps calling you to get you to come back. He brings guys back who have been out of college for three or four years. Look at me, I am back this semester. I only need fifteen more credits before I graduate. He is a prime example of what a coach or boss should be. He cares about everybody.

Gordon Brown talks about his recent interactions with Coach Snyder.

> After I finished playing I came back and got my degree, and then entered the police academy. When I would come back to talk with Coach Snyder, I wanted to talk about how the team was doing. He kept saying, "Did you graduate from the academy yet?" All he wanted to talk about was how I was doing in school and when I thought I would graduate. I know he was proud of me when I graduated from the police academy and started to work at Kansas State.

Mike "Crash" Ekeler agrees that Coach Snyder thinks of each player as an individual and treats them all fairly.

> I was a walk on at Kansas State. No one expected me to play much. After about the third game of the season Coach came into our meeting and said, "All right, some of you want to play and are putting out the effort. Others are not. If there is someone who is not playing that thinks he should be playing tell the coaches, and we will see what you've got." That week in practice we were getting after it pretty good. I was on the scout special team kickoff coverage squad. I ran down the field and knocked some people down. When I got up I was going nuts. One of our better players got hurt on the play. I heard Coach Snyder yelling, and I thought, great, he is going to kick me off the team. He came up, grabbed my arm and said "Mike Ekeler, I like you. You are going to play for me." He kind of took me

under his wing from then on. He is almost like a second father to me.

Kansas City Chiefs player Kevin Lockett continues to be impressed with Coach Snyder's fairness.

He is a stickler for the rules. I can very distinctly remember him laying down rules and guidelines about how we should and should not act throughout the season. He always told us that there would be serious consequences if we broke the rules. It is natural for us to wonder if the rules would apply to everyone, or if the punishment depended on who got caught. I clearly remember something that happened early in my career. One of our great players, a "superstar," violated one of the team rules. Coach Snyder treated him exactly as if he were a walk on. That player did not play in the next game. Coach not only earned a lot of respect from the players, but reinforced the fact that everyone is treated equally. There are no prima donnas and no outcasts on Coach Snyder's teams.

?

How do you feel about multicultural education at the college level?
Leo Prieto
Class of '99, Garden City, Kansas

I strongly support it. This is what we do. Football is a game of mutual sacrifices which transcend all possible diversities.
Coach Snyder

When it comes to honoring and respecting diversity, Coach Snyder has a criteria that everybody understands. Everyone is being evaluated by the same standard. Regardless of your individual differences in race, background, or ability level, you will not be surprised by any of his decisions. He demands a great deal out of each student. By definition he is not discriminating and has the same high expectations for all.

Sean Snyder recalls, "Playing for him I learned more about his love for the game. The one thing that I appreciate more than anything is that he made me earn everything. He never gave me something for nothing." Former player Matt Garber recalls that,

> One example of how seriously he takes the team concept can be seen in what he did after the Coca Cola Bowl we played in Tokyo, Japan. Andre Coleman was named the K-State MVP of the game. The people running the game told Coach Snyder that only he and Andre needed to stay around for the post game festivities. Coach Snyder told them, "If you don't want my football team, then you don't want me. This is a team." This act of team support continued to mean a lot to the players throughout the year because his actions showed that we were all going to be treated alike, and that our team demanded respect.

Greg Sharpe, the "Voice of the Wildcats," observed that what happened in Tokyo is very consistent with how Coach Snyder operates.

> Each year there will be players who are legitimate candidates for significant post-season recognition. Coach Snyder will not place one player over another. He creates an opportunity for the athlete to excel, but he is not going to push one player above another. That is just not his style or his theory of a team. He will let the players' actions on the field do the talking. Although he will not mount a campaign to get a player an award, he does create the opportunity for the player to excel, but he will not overly publicize the player.

Other professionals share Coach Snyder's belief in maximizing individual strengths. Steve Dorfman admires Snyder's commitment to education.

> As far as the military, and probably all organizations are concerned, education is the key. You need to be aware that people are different. People come from different backgrounds, but that doesn't make one person any better than another or any person worse than another person. You need to learn how to draw on a person's strengths to make it all work together. If you can do that, you've succeeded. If you can do that, not only as a leader,

but as a person who is part of that group, I think you have succeeded as well because you can learn something from everyone. This attitude will allow you to break down any preconceived notions about race or income or any other individual difference.

Businessman Dennis Mullin believes that,

Being sensitive to each person that you are working with increases the opportunity of providing meaningful leadership. You will have problems in any organization if you try to take the new person and attempt to fit him or her into a rigid system without understanding and having empathy regarding their background and previous experience. The world is changing more rapidly for our youth than ever before. If you're not willing to listen and understand that, you will not achieve long-term success. Bill's long-term success is partially due to the fact that he understands the people that he is working with. He listens, adjusts, and modifies his program to accommodate the changes in his players and their individual strengths and weaknesses. In doing so, he doesn't bend from his overall principles. He understands what each player needs in order to be able to teach him.

Robert DeBruyn, Manhattan business leader, believes that Coach Snyder

Is very good at identifying strengths. He recognizes and capitalizes on each player's strength. It is unlikely that someone will follow you if they don't believe in you and trust that you recognize their strengths. All people can learn and all people have a gift, but it takes special people who can find that gift. Coach Snyder does not write people off. He consistently demonstrates that he believes in improvement.

Larry Kramer, former assistant coach, believes that one of the clearest indications of Coach Snyder's belief in each person's ability to improve is his history of awarding scholarships to former walk on players.

Quite a few "walk on" youngsters have earned scholarships since he's been at Kansas State. He recognizes their individual talents. Every two or three weeks, all staff review the personnel board and determine what's best for the player and what's best for the team. Coach Snyder is very creative in the use of individual talent.

A clear example of Coach Snyder's respect for the individual and his assumption that each person should be given the opportunity to make a contribution to the program is seen in the relationship that he had with assistant coach Bob Cope. Coach Cope was diagnosed with cancer during the 1996-97 season. He continued to coach on the field until he needed to be hospitalized; however, his coaching did not end there. The coaching staff wanted to make sure that Coach Cope understood that he was a valuable member of the program. Coach Cope continued to be an important member of the coaching staff until very near his death. Coach Snyder went to see Cope every day, taking the game plans and asking him for advice.

Leadership Lesson Number Seven

Respect for diversity is best achieved by ensuring that everyone is focusing on a common goal.

Women's Basketball coach Deb Patterson believes that today the football teams at major universities are microcosms of society. She values Coach Snyder's understanding of the complexities and opportunities that diverse players bring to the team.

Thirty or forty years ago, "big time" football programs mostly consisted of white, middle or lower class athletes. There has been an obvious and dramatic shift in the opportunities for a much broader range of people to take part. I think it was much easier for Knute Rockne to be successful at Notre Dame in his day, than it is for Bill Snyder to be successful today. It really speaks highly of the ability of leaders like Coach Snyder, who are able to recognize the differences that exist on their teams and still mold one hundred and twenty youngsters into a cohesive team.

How do you successfully bring together a group of people as diverse as the football team? There are rural kids and urban kids; Kansans and those from out of state; whites, blacks, Asians, etc. How do you get them past their stereotypes and prejudices so that they can unite as a team?

Trent Benisch
Class of '01, Sharon Springs, Kansas

Football is a game of mutual sacrifices which transcend all possible diversities. Those who fail to recognize and respond to this quickly fall by the wayside.

Coach Snyder

In dealing with athletics, particularly in football, we deal with large numbers of people. Just by the sheer number of one hundred and twenty young people there is quite obviously significant diversity. Football has a tendency to transcend all areas of diversity. It is important in football, and in the larger world of work, that you are able to communicate well with all members of our diverse society.

On our team, as well as in most urban businesses, there are white youngsters who may come from a rural community and have never been in the same building with a black youngster. By the same token, you have black youngsters from large urban areas who may never have been in an educational building with a white individual other than a teacher. In our program we work very hard at understanding and responding to differences. What helps us do that more than anything else is that we have a common cause and a common bond that we can all relate to. All of our players can relate to the bottom line approach:"Why are we here?" and "What is it that has brought us together?"

Each individual in the program has the opportunity to draw together and form a common bond. It is only then that we begin to learn about diversity, and gain a better understanding of how we might better deal with those individual differences. I don't think that we become successful, or have a successful program, or do a successful job of guiding young people by first attempting to get them to understand individual differences and then come together and join this common bond. I think it's just the opposite. I think we create a common bond, and through that, we realize these are the things that have to take place. For us, it goes back to our sixteen goals. At the very top it's "Unity — To come together like never before in the history of college football." By being part of the team, each individual learns that in order to be individually successful, and for the team to be successful, we have to come together. We have to become unified. Accordingly, each individual must come to understand their inter-relatedness. Our program brings people together and through that process, they learn about each other's differences and they learn to accept and respect these differences.

Bob Snell agrees: "If you can have a common goal, then many of the differences become less significant and less important. Coach Snyder does this very well. Certainly, if you look at the home address of his players, where these youngsters come from, there is a great deal of diversity. Actually there's more diversity economically, within race, than there is across race."

Coach Snyder believes that lessons of sensitivity to diversity are learned through participation in the football program and former players agree. *Youngsters who have gone through our program come back and indicate that they have learned to recognize differences between individuals and through our program they have learned how to accept and deal with diversity. For example, I am convinced that youngsters in our program are better prepared to deal with diversity in the work place as a result of the experiences they have had in the Kansas State University football program.*

Clearly these lessons could eventually be learned on the job, but the learning process may result in experiences that could be detrimental to their careers. Our program provides a spring board, or a transition to the work place. A lot of what we do here is education. Although some students may go into the classroom and have difficulty the first semester, most eventually learn how to become students. They learn how to study. They learn what is expected of them on a college campus that wasn't expected of them at the high school level. They gradually learn how to fit into the system. By the second semester, they learn that there are prices to be paid for not studying. The same is true in our program. Emotional maturity and sensitivity to diversity are lessons that are only learned over time. These lessons are learned here.

Quentin Neujahr believes the strongest message Coach Snyder gives is that, "We are all into this together, and we need each other to survive." Neujahr remembers a game against North Texas State in 1989. "We beat them with a last-minute drive. We were not black or white, we beat them as a team. We learned that players must stick together as a team and depend on each other."

Sean Snyder observes that, "One of the things that we talk about a great deal is that we are a family. Negative attitudes about race have been reduced significantly over time."

Leadership Lesson Number Eight

Discriminatory attitudes, behaviors, or statements have no place in an ethical and fair organization and will negatively impact the successful attainment of goals.

The football program represents one of the most racially diverse units on the campus. Coach Snyder's success in building a cohesive unit and his explicit statements of what constitutes a fair and ethical organization are a model of a proven strategy. When we asked Coach Snyder what he would do if he or his staff became aware of one of his players using racist or otherwise inappropriate language, he told us about a recent incident that clearly illustrates how an organization can foster equity while demonstrating that racism will not be tolerated. *A young player from rural white America entered our program, and all of a sudden it was a whole different world for him. He had no experience with diversity, and was not prepared to deal with it. It came to our attention that he was using inappropriate language, racially charged language, when he was outside the program. Even though this inappropriate behavior did not take place in the context of the football program, it is behavior that we will not tolerate. I called him into my office and made it very clear to him that his language and attitude was unacceptable. I explained to him why it was unacceptable and how it impacted our goals and vision. Not only is it intolerable in our program, but it is intolerable in our society. I explained to him that if he had any hope of having success in the workplace, he would have to modify his attitudes and behaviors.*

As a result of our conversations, language took on a significantly different meaning for him. I told him that to remain with our program he would have to immediately change his ways. He has remained in our program, and has fit in well. He understands what happened. He altered his behavior immediately. However, it took a little more time for him to understand why the new behavior was appropriate. This is the way it often happens. He knew that he had broken a rule, but he was really not sure why the rule was established. Today, he will tell you how foolish he was, and how foolish his beliefs were. Racial discrimination is wrong and it will not be tolerated on our team.

This is a good example of the way that organizational values shape the behavior of individuals in the program. There are some values that are so important to the organization that if someone can't accept those values, then this is probably not the place for him. It also relates to the similarities between a coach and a parent. Most parents would attempt to correct without destroying the relationship or driving the child away.

?

Will there ever be a place for women in college football?
Aubrey Abbott
Class of '98, Larned, Kansas

To what degree I am not certain, but I believe it is on the horizon. I met a young woman who had played football for a junior college team in California and I invited her to help me coach the East-West Shrine game in 1998. She is dedicated to a coaching career and has had some offers. Today you see women sportscasters on major networks and there are numerous female athletic trainers in college football.
Coach Snyder

The football program's commitment to fairness and equity are highly valued by both players and the larger community. Former linebacker Kirby Hocutt recalls that, "It does not matter if you are a white or black. It doesn't matter if you are Hispanic or any other ethnic group, you are going to be treated equally by Coach and his coaching staff."

Various K-State administrators are also aware and appreciative of Coach Snyder's stand for fairness and against discrimination. Kathy Greene recalls that,

> When Coach Snyder came to K-State, there were not that many minority players on the football team. I was surprised that the team itself was predominately white. Snyder immediately hired two African-American coaches, and they worked well together. I'm an African-American woman and I was impressed. I told my sons that Coach Snyder would be very sensitive to their needs, which influenced their decision to go to Kansas State.

Leaders Must Promote Equity and Fairness

According to former defensive lineman Tim Colston, Coach Snyder:

> Laid the foundation for how we were going to act toward people. While we were in the program we learned to treat everyone in the program as a member of our family. The people that pass through the Kansas State football program have a foundation of treating people fairly. While you are in the program you see just about everything as far as personalities, races, backgrounds, all under one roof. When you leave the program you are more likely to be able to deal with diversity than people who have not had this experience. We leave having had a chance to become friends with people we might not otherwise have gotten to know. We get to understand about differences without being so judgmental.

Reggie McGowan, Director of KSU Upward Bound, affirms that Coach Snyder is not passive about equity. Whether Snyder is on campus or off-campus his message is the same. "He really emphasized the value of diversity and the need for the alumni to become culturally aware."

Mordean Taylor-Archer often has the opportunity of working with Coach Snyder on student-related projects.

> We were recently talking about possible entertainment alternatives to Aggieville, and we were particularly focusing on the social needs of black athletes. We were brainstorming ideas that would help black athletes become better connected to the campus. The thing that was really very heart-warming for me was the fact that the coach was so receptive to the idea of our having some kind of mentorship program for black athletes. I think that the coach has done a really stellar job of recruiting a diverse group of athletes, and of supporting that group of athletes. He demonstrates his commitment to equity in the selection of quarterbacks. Clearly, Jonathan Beasley and Michael Bishop have helped break the stereotype that black athletes can't quarterback.

It is very clear that the respect that Snyder shows to his players is reciprocated. Provost Jim Coffman tells of an event that took place while he and his wife were attending a bowl game. "Coach clearly has the respect of all the players. Sharon and I were in the elevator with two players several hours after the team's victory in the Fiesta Bowl. As we traveled between floors one of the players asked the other if he was going to go downtown and celebrate. The second player said he needed to press his pants before going out. They said if it was important to Coach Snyder that they looked sharp, then it was important to them."

Veryl Switzer, Associate Athletics Director, believes that Coach Snyder, "Has a lot to do with whether or not the various races get along in a healthy association. Students watch those that are in control. They watch Coach Snyder to see how he is going to conduct himself regarding the race issue. I think that has made a big difference as to how they conduct themselves. I have not detected any racial tension on the team under Coach Snyder. He relates well to the needs of black student athletes."

Switzer notes that Coach Snyder is fair with all of his athletes.

Students can't point a finger and say that the coach is playing favorites. The best proof of how he treats people of color is that we no longer have black athletes discouraging other black athletes from coming to Kansas State. Whereas in the past, we would have black students saying, "You don't want to come here. I am here because I am stuck here and now I don't have any other choice." This has never occurred since Snyder has been here, even before the team started winning.

Leadership Lesson Number Nine

Ethical organizations are based on loyalty and service to individual members, as well as to the greater community.

Service to others is a consistent theme that runs through Coach Snyder's leadership philosophy. Although he constantly encourages others to join him in focusing on assisting our youth, he is very private about his own acts of service. When we specifically asked why he spends so much time talking to school children, visiting hospitals and retirement communities, and serving on community organizations, he replied that, *My intent when I address a group of young people or adults is to send a message that will have an impact on their behavior, that will cause them to do something in a positive nature. I encourage children and young adults to try to do some positive things in their life. That is the primary reason I am interested in working on this book — to help students become stronger leaders. I think that if every adult group would focus on helping our youth in a specific way, that our problems would be significantly reduced. Then pretty soon your actions would not only decrease the negative, but would increase the positive. I think it is important to get young people to develop leadership skills so that they can go out into the community and provide leadership aimed at improving society.*

Coach Snyder maintains a very heavy speaking schedule. *Every year I try to reduce the number of speeches that I give, but I can't seem to do it. When I accept invitations, my first choice is to try to be in a position to impact children and young people. My second priority is the various constituency groups that support Kansas State University. I usually only accept invitations from corporations and service organizations when I believe that by speaking to them I might encourage them to make a positive impact on youth.*

Leaders Have a Duty to Contribute
to the Well Being of the Community

During the process of writing this book, we have had the opportunity to hear Coach Snyder speak quite a few times. Although he adapts each speech to the unique experiences of his audience, his basic message is the same. In every one of his speeches there is a call for action. As he speaks, it is absolutely clear that he did not take time from his coaching responsibilities to talk about coaching, or to tell football stories. Snyder approaches each speech with the same seriousness that he prepares for a football game. For example, when he spoke at the Kansas Press Association conference he ended his remarks by challenging each publisher to go home and dedicate his or her paper to improving the lives of children in their communities. He directly confronted these community leaders with the fact that they had power in their communities, and they should use that power to make a difference in the lives of the young people.

It is encouraging to see that people listen when Coach Snyder speaks. Steve Johnson, Lawrence business person, was an exhibitor at the Kansas Press Association meeting. At the conclusion of Coach Snyder's speech, Johnson commented that the most important point contained in Snyder's speech was "about the kids that are coming up through the schools, and how we have a responsibility to provide leadership for them. When I go back to my company I will keep in mind that everything we do has an impact on the children."

Coach Snyder accepts many more invitations than we would have imagined. *I'm part of Kansas State, so I want to promote the university. I'm part of Manhattan, and I want to promote the community. I'm part of Kansas and I want to promote Kansas. When I travel outside of Kansas, I take every opportunity to talk about the accomplishments of the larger university. Unfortunately, there is only one section of the newspaper that doesn't go unread, and that's the sports page. This is true everywhere across the country. When we win a ball game it's going to be in every major paper in the country. Yet, Kansas State is only now beginning to be recognized for its tremendous record of academic achievement, but still gets very limited coverage outside of the state. Consequently, I share President Wefald's commitment to take every opportunity to help people understand the larger Kansas State University success story. The outstanding academic achievements of our faculty and students is far more important and impressive than the accomplishments of any athletic team.*

The impact of Coach Snyder's commitment to service is found throughout the football program. Players are encouraged to become involved in some form of service to the community. The impact of this philosophy can be seen in the comments of former defensive end John Butler.

Coach Snyder does the right thing for the right reasons. He is never looking for publicity for himself. A good example of this can be seen in something that happened during the flood in Manhattan in 1993. Several team members got together, on their own, and went out to help sandbag. About thirty guys went out and helped. We went back on a second day and as we came around a corner, there was Coach Snyder in the back of a truck. He was handing out sand bags. I thought, "What is going on here?" He had on a t-shirt and shorts, and he was working hard. We saved a couple houses. It was really kind of neat to see him working right along with the other members of the community. He wasn't giving orders. He was pitching in and helping, like everyone else.

Provost Coffman is in a unique position to observe Coach Snyder's service to the total university. "His leadership and support of the Friends of the Library is very significant. He has directly helped raise a great deal of money for the library. He knows that, because of the success of the football team, he has the opportunity of helping to raise funds for other areas of the university."

Mike Holen, Dean of the College of Education, concurs.

Coach Snyder is a genuine supporter of the university's academic mission. The contributions he has made to our Leadership Studies program, as well as the library have been extremely significant. He also clearly has broader interests in developing young people as individuals and as societal leaders. On a more personal note, I had heart surgery during the busiest time of the football season, and Coach Snyder was one of the first to call me and to follow my progress, and continue to wish me well. He has a real sense of affection for people. He has a strong desire to help people succeed and to celebrate with them when they do. I don't know if there is a better definition of a teacher than that.

?

How do you instill a sense of responsibility in your players for on- and off-field behavior?

> Patrick Carney
> Class '98, Prairie Village, Kansas

A commitment to the success of a team effort promotes individual responsibility. Therefore, we ask for a strong commitment from each player in our program to make decisions based upon the goals and priorities of their team. A system is also in place that disciplines those who act irresponsibly.

> *Coach Snyder*

As a leader who is training other leaders, Coach Snyder's personal actions serve as a very significant role model for his players. Matt Miller, graduate assistant, recalls, "One week Coach is taking players to retirement community and the next week to the Veterans Hospital. He teaches players about the broader world. He constantly models the ideal of helping others."

When Coach Snyder visits a school or a retirement community, he always takes some of his players with him. After a recent visit to a local long-term care facility, its administrator, Phillip M. Levi, wrote a letter to the editor of the *Manhattan Mercury* thanking Coach Snyder and his players for the visit. Excerpts from the letter document both the intent and the impact of Leadership Lesson Nine:

> Thank you, Coach, for the excitement you generated. . . . The players' confidence, dedication and the obvious enjoyment and appreciation they all expressed to be associated with a football program like the one you have created was evident. It was when you had the players roam the room signing autographs, having their pictures taken, first with kids then with residents, families, volunteers and staff that the magic took over.
>
> These young gentlemen were wonderful ambassadors for KSU. Mark Simoneau, Jeff Kelly, Michael Bishop, Travis Ochs and Martez Wesley were so genuine, friendly, kind and willing to give of themselves that the whole room warmed up. Everyone had to have a poster for a grandchild (or was it to

hang up in their room?) Most had at least one player's signature. . . .

Elementary school children in Manhattan also benefit from Coach Snyder's lessons. Katha Hurt, elementary school principal, reports that after a recent visit to her school by Coach Snyder and some of his team, she followed up with her students in order to determine what they recalled from his talk. She was impressed by how many of the students were able to discuss setting goals and trying to get better every day.

As teachers, we often wonder if we are making any difference in the lives of our students. Often students pass through our classes and we never know what they have learned that they will carry with them into the future. Working on this book reminded us that one never knows which of our words or actions will be remembered and make a difference. This idea was brought to our attention as we spoke with former team member Matt Garber, whose last year at Kansas State was 1992. We asked him to tell us his most vivid memory of his time playing for Coach Snyder. We anticipated that he would recall an exciting game moment or a "thrill of victory" story. Instead, he told us the following:

> During my junior year there was a young Manhattan boy who was very ill, who had maybe less than a month to live. Coach Snyder invited him to come to practice and spend some time with the team. It was clear that the boy was having a great time. Several weeks later we were traveling to a game out of state, and the coach learned that the little boy had passed away. It really put football into perspective for all of us. I think we all felt good knowing that our time with this little boy was so important to him. This event brought more meaning to football, to know that what we were doing was so important to others. It really showed us how important it is to show that you care about people and to appreciate the blessings that you have.

Leaders who Demonstrate Loyalty Inspire Loyalty

In addition to modeling service to others, Coach Snyder demonstrates the importance of loyalty. Coach Larry Kramer speaks of Coach Snyder as ". . . really a very loyal guy. Of all his positive traits, I think I admire his loyalty most; and I think he appreciates loyalty the most in others, too.

He's just an old-fashioned guy; you can count on him."

As we talked with former players, most mentioned how important it was to them that they knew that, no matter what happened, they could depend on him. According to Kirby Hocutt, "Coach Snyder is not only loyal to us when we played for him, but he continues to be. I know that he has written a reference for me to every employer I have had since college."

Snyder demonstrates his loyalty to his players in many concrete ways. The well being of his players is of prime importance to him. Although he has drawn criticism from the media for his refusal to distribute an injury report, he believes *It is only common sense to understand that by announcing the injury status of a player you might be exposing that player to further injury. Additionally, such an announcement would allow opponents to modify their game plans to take advantage of the injury.* Coach Snyder also has another reason for not wishing to announce injury reports. He believes that one of the biggest problems in college athletics today is the corrupting influence of gambling, and that announcing injuries fosters this destructive practice.

Theoretical Context

Leaders have the power to influence the organization's ethics through their own behavior and through their reaction to the behavior of others. Coach Snyder establishes ethical ground rules for the football program that help to create a positive climate. As everyone in the football program comes to understand the ground rules and can trust each other to comply with the common ethical code, there is greater respect among all people in the program. Coach Snyder exercises ethical leadership by being truthful, fair, and consistent in all of his relationships. He also reinforces the acceptable limits for ethical behavior as he manages the interactions and dealings of the program members. Therefore, ethical leadership is not something that only emerges in times of crisis or an obvious moral dilemma, but is an integral part of his everyday leadership.

Coach Snyder's ethical leadership is very consistent with the four psychological components of ethical behavior that authors Rest and Narvaez, in *Moral Development in the Professions*, have identified as: moral sensitivity, moral judgment, moral motivation, and moral character. "Moral sensitivity" refers to our awareness of how our actions affect other people; Coach Snyder demonstrates this trait when he makes it clear that he will not tolerate racist language or behavior from any of his players. "Moral judgment" involves the process of deciding what is right and wrong in a specific situation. Coach Snyder consistently teaches his players that they must work toward their goals, "the right way." Bob Snell and others confirmed the high degree of integrity in the football program at Kansas State. "Moral motivation" refers to the importance given to moral values that may be in competition with other values; Snyder will not break rules to win a game or to help a player. "Moral character" refers to the leader's practice of ethical leadership.

One of the clearest places to see Snyder's ethical leadership is in his passionate commitment to equality and inclusiveness. Today, almost all organizations are reevaluating their organizational cultures and their practices to ensure that all members are treated fairly. In *The New Leaders: Leadership Diversity in America*, Ann Morrison of the Center for Creative Leadership lists education, enforcement, and exposure as the essential components for diversity appreciation programs. Frequently, institutions focus on education and enforcement, and ignore exposure. Coach Snyder's approach is to firmly enforce a strong anti-discrimination policy. He then guides his players to become a team with a common goal, while at the same time helping them develop mutual respect. After this exposure to diversity has occurred, he initiates a more comprehensive education program about racial diversity. This model deserves careful consideration by anyone who is working to promote diversity in corporations, agencies, or educational institutions.

For further study of equality, ethics, and diversity we recommend:

Kanungo, R., and Mendonca, M. (1996). *Ethical Dimensions of Leadership*. London: Sage.

Morrison, A. M. (1996). *The New Leaders: Leadership Diversity in America*. San Francisco: Jossey-Bass.

Rest, J. R., and Narvaez, P. (1994). *Moral Development in the Professions*. Hillsdale, NJ: Erlbaum.

Chapter Three

Communication

S UCCESSFUL LEADERSHIP does not occur without effective communication. This chapter illustrates Coach Snyder's philosophy and techniques of verbal and nonverbal communication. Chapter Three includes four Leadership Lessons that address the issues of feedback, repetition, explaining, and storytelling.

Lesson Ten explores methods of giving honest and direct feedback in a positive manner.

Lesson Eleven provides specific suggestions for how to effectively teach a new concept.

Lesson Twelve discusses the importance of providing reasons and explanations for your decisions.

Lesson Thirteen describes the powerful technique of storytelling.

Leadership Lesson Number Ten

All communication should be open, direct, and positive.

Every leader faces the challenge of providing frank and timely feedback while at the same time being perceived as open to the comments and concerns of others. Coach Snyder's style incorporates openness and direct feedback in a supportive environment.

Allow for Both Structured and Informal Feedback

We encourage both formal and informal feedback from our players. During the course of the year, I attempt to meet with the player representatives every Monday. Sometimes we brainstorm about their issues and concerns. At other meetings we follow up on issues that have been raised at previous meetings. In general, the meetings have two primary purposes. One is to ensure that we coaches are aware of any concerns or problems that exist. The other is to have a vehicle we can use to disseminate information to the rest of the team. Meeting on Monday allows us to start the week fresh with an informal meeting. Because time is such a demanding element for players in our program, the meetings are usually held on the field after a practice or after a workout. By having the meetings then, we are able to reduce the amount of time the player representatives have to spend. If you are not careful about such issues as time, you will defeat the purpose of the meeting. Pretty soon nobody would want to be a player representative if you intruded on their time, which is very precious to them.

Regular Meetings Encourage Participants to Share Concerns

I take all of the players' concerns seriously. If it's important enough for them to want to talk to me about it, then I pay strict attention. We're going to pursue it, and we're not going to close anything off. For example, recently, the player representatives and I met with some other people concerning our team meals. There were some things the players wanted changed. You have to realize that for a nineteen- or twenty-year-old foot-ball player, eating is one of the biggest priorities in his life. This was an important issue for the players, consequently it was an important issue for me. When the player representatives brought the issues to me, we sat down and talked about it. I made sure that they felt comfortable expressing their honest feelings and required that they offer suggestions for improvement. I collected all of the information and then I met with the people who were responsible for the team meals and we discussed the players' concerns. I then brought our training table people and our player representatives together and let the player representatives talk directly with the people responsible for the training table. It was decided to develop a question-naire and distribute it to all of the players in order to arrive at a consen-sus. The results of the questionnaire were presented and specific changes were implemented. The people responsible for the training table are very good people, were very responsive to our players' concerns, and were willing to work with us.

Having been in a position to observe Coach Snyder for over 20 years, former coach Larry Kramer comments, "Coach Snyder listens to his play-ers and his assistant coaches better than any other coach I have ever worked with. He learns from them and calls them in and visits with them regularly. There's no question that he is the boss, but his coaches have a lot of freedom on Saturday."

Others also appreciate his openness to suggestions and his ability to handle conflict, often before it arises. Matt Miller believes that Coach Snyder gives his assistants a lot of authority to make decisions. "He will even take suggestions from me, a graduate assistant, or anyone else who has a suggestion for improvement. He understands that seven minds work-ing together are smarter than one working alone. If you spend time in the Vanier Complex you will notice that Coach has players in his office every day."

Coach Snyder has a systematic process to allow dissent and criticism to come up. He appears to deal with conflict by getting out in front of it so that he is not surprised. Many conflicts occur when we are caught off guard, we get defensive, and we feel as though we have to fight. Coach Snyder prepares himself so that he is not often surprised. He is not afraid to say that he does not have all of the answers. He promotes frequent and honest feedback by consistently asking for it.

Snyder has turned his philosophy of open and honest communication into the standard operating procedure in his program. In many organizations, information only flows from the top down. In Coach Snyder's program, he constantly seeks information from everyone in the program while frequently sharing information about what is going on in the program.

? What separates good public speakers from poor public speakers?
Chris Smither
Burlington, Kansas

Personally, I believe that strength in communication is created through sincerity.

Coach Snyder

In addition to facilitating the sharing of information, an open communication process also provides support and encouragement for members of the organization. Coach Snyder takes every opportunity to provide positive reinforcement. Coach Kramer reports, "Regardless of what has happened in the game that day, Coach Snyder never lets a player leave the locker room feeling down."

I strongly believe in positive reinforcement. We always want to be able to tell a young man that he did well. There is a pristine honesty about athletics that may be unique. Everything you do is on videotape — everything. You can't escape it. Youngsters meet with the coaches on Monday afternoon and watch themselves, and die a thousand deaths because they are exposed. They are up there and just absolutely exposed. If they did well, it will certainly present itself and a coach will provide the applause that says that's good. However, good and bad, right and wrong, it's all up on the monitor. It's very cut and dried in that regard. Just as players are identified and applauded for doing what is right and appropriate, they are also identified when they don't perform as well. Therein lies accepting the responsibility for success as well as failure.

Former players remember and appreciate Coach Snyder's sincere interest in their well being. Former quarterback Chris Cobb recalls,

I can't remember him ever taking credit for anything. He always gave the team and his assistant coaches all the credit for our success. He has a way of communicating that really gets your attention. One day I was having a bad day punting and he came over and put his arm around me and said, "It's going to be all right. Just think about what you know how to do and concentrate." He never wanted you to give up, or take the easy way out. He would get a bunch of "yeses" before he would get a "no." You would confirm that, "Yes, I can do this; Yes, I've had better days; Yes, I've had good days." He would get your mind to say yes, yes, yes, so you would kind of forget about the problem. By the time it is all over with you have confidence again. It's just like life, you can have self doubt. And when you start doubting yourself you are doomed. He could always sense when you were doubting yourself and were frustrated.

He could also sense when you were not meeting your expectations, and he would always come over and give you some specific suggestion to improve. He would say something like, "When you threw that pass, your foot was not pointed at the target," or, "Your release point is a little high." Although he is an ultra technician, he understands that when you are too technical your mind can get in your way. He has the ability to get you back into the flow of having fun. He would keep you from over analyzing.

When I did something right as quarterback, or got off a good punt, he would say, "I knew you could do it, because you did it once. Now, I expect you to do it like that all the time." I think of this process of positive reinforcement today at my job. Whether I am managing other people or doing something myself, I believe that you can keep repeating your successes. I learned that, by striving for consistency you will get your maximum performance.

Mark Porter observes that, "Coach Snyder's players learn from what Coach Snyder does. His 'never say die' attitude sets the tone for what they do. Because Coach Snyder perceives himself as a winner and perceives you as a winner, you begin to perceive yourself as a winner too."

Leadership Lesson Number Eleven

Successful communication is accomplished through continual repetition of an individualized message.

On Coach Snyder's effectiveness as a teacher, Director of Athletics Max Urick reflects that,

> All the great coaches know what is important to the youngsters they coach. They must know what is on their players minds. It doesn't mean that they necessarily agree with it, or that they can change it, but they must stay current with the changing culture and make certain adaptations. Coach Snyder stays current. By frequently meeting with the player representatives he knows what is working and what is not working. He is able to anticipate problems before they get out of hand.

One of Coach Snyder's most effective communication strategies is repeating the same message with the specific needs and communication styles of his audience in mind. *Over a period of time, some people hear me say the same things over and over again. Each time they hear the same general theme. I am a believer in repetition, repetition, repetition. Everything in our program is based on the assumption that repetition breeds success. If there are fifth year seniors in our program who are making the same mistakes that they made when they entered our program, you would have to question our ability to teach and coach. It all boils down to the need for repetition in order to get it done.* Veryl Switzer concurs, "He is very consistent. He keeps repeating the same message and pretty soon you see his student-athletes emulating him."

Constant Modification and Adaption is Critical to Effective Leadership

We are constantly modifying what we do, if we believe there is a better way. For example, we modified how we approach the task of discussing our goals with our players. Although we believe that all of our goals are valuable and should be reinforced, we came to the realization that our method of reinforcing these goals with our players was not as effective with our upper class students as it was with the newer students. Because our older students had sat through several very similar presentations, we decided that there was a danger of them thinking "Been there, done that."

It used to take me an hour and a half, over two days of meetings with our players, to go through what we believe are very significant goals and values for our football team. Because most of the players in our program have been here for an extended period of time, I no longer repeat this information. Now I take the players who are new to our program and go through the comprehensive presentation and discussion. However, we don't want our upperclassman to forget our goals. So we focus on individual goals with them on a daily basis. For example, we might present one or two goals a day (improvement or responsibility or accountability). Or, I might address one or two goals in an evening meeting. I might initiate our practice with just one concept for fifteen seconds before we start practice. By visiting with them for fifteen to twenty seconds about each concept they stay fresh on their minds. In this way, each practice reinforces one of our goals.

Identifying Success is Critical for Improvement

It is important to help people identify their successes. It is also important to help them identify what actions they took that allowed them to be successful. Virtually every ball game we have played has been significant for succeeding games. By looking back at individual games and specific incidents in individual games, we are able to demonstrate to the current players the relationship between actions and consequences. This process enhances the credibility of our coaches and allows the current athletes to see material evidence of past success. This allows the coaches to explain the why, what, how and when of success. By pointing to past successes, it is more likely that the current athlete will follow directions and improve.

Motivating college students is not as easy as it might have once been. Other educational leaders who work with college students every day admire Coach Snyder's ability to understand and motivate college students. As Dean Holen notes, "Coach Snyder has an exceptional understanding of how to work incrementally with young people and make issues concrete for them."

Leadership Lesson Number Twelve

It is important to explain in detail the reason behind decisions and directives, if possible.

Open Communication Enhances a Leader's Credibility

Open communication not only enhances communication and builds relationships, but raises the probability that future decisions will be accepted even when explanations are not reasonable or feasible. *I think I have always given people the reasons for my actions, and explained why I demanded a certain behavior. I tell them my plan. I explain that this is what we want to do. Here is how we are going to do it, and here is the projected outcome. I also tell them, "If we do this this way for this reason, here's what we should be able to expect as the projected outcome." I think that is important for a team, or a staff, or a company to be able to understand the big picture. When you can demonstrate the truth of your words by being able to show them how the plan has worked in the past, it will be more likely that you will be believed and followed.*

Today, more than ever before, motivating student athletes depends on an ability to communicate. Open and honest communication increases the probability of receiving a positive response from the student athlete. We attempt to provide the information in such a way that they understand exactly what is requested and required of them. We also communicate exactly how their actions will impact them and what the outcome is going to be. We also explain why it is important that the actions taken be executed in a particular way. It is very important to be open with information.

How do you demote or discipline a player so he does not get discouraged?

Michael Johnson
Class of '99, Garden City, Kansas

We would allow him to know that he is capable of much more and can achieve at the level he aspires if he has a plan to eliminate the action(s) that brought about the disciplinary action. We will help him with establishing that plan if he will make a commitment to it.
Coach Snyder

You must build trust through open communication before a situation arises where you can't give ample explanation for your decisions. If you have good reasons for what you do, you explain these reasons, and if the consequences are generally what you told them to expect, your followers will follow you even when they don't know why they are being asked to take some action.

There has to be a foundation built that allows trust to motivate action. There will be times when a player may say, "I don't know why we are doing this," or even, "I don't want to do this." At these times, if trust has been built, you hope the player will say, "I trust this guy. I trust what he is telling me, because what he has told me in the past has always worked out the way he said it would." I'm pretty confident that youngsters, and perhaps most of us, need to have faith and trust in our leaders.

Leadership Lesson Number Thirteen

Storytelling and providing visual images are effective means of communication and leadership.

Telling stories is a way of carrying the history of the organization from generation to generation. Stories can be used for motivation, to put the present into perspective, to inspire, and to give confidence. Coach Snyder frequently uses stories to reinforce a point or motivate his players. The first time we visited with Coach Snyder we noticed a framed production cell from the original *Pinocchio* movie on the wall next to his desk. It is our observation that Coach Snyder seldom, if ever, does anything by accident. Therefore, we were very interested to learn why he selected this particular picture.

Coach Snyder replied with the following story: *That production cell was given to me by a very close friend. My favorite movie is Pinocchio. When people ask me why, I don't hesitate to tell them that it is because of the compassion that Gepetto had for people, and Pinocchio in particular. It was a movie that I saw several times. I took every one of my five children to see the movie. When Pinocchio came out in videotape, I bought every one I could get my hands on. I still send a copy to friends of a certain age. All my children have a copy of it. It meant more than just a shoemaker with compassion for people, but it was also his craftsmanship with a piece of wood and what he was able to do with not much to work with, what he was able to create from it. It was the significance of a young person learning how to grow up and mature and go through some difficult times and make some mistakes and, with the help of others, land on his feet. I became attracted to it because I thought it had such a great message for young people.*

Coach Snyder uses stories to make the process of decision making more tangible for his players. By using metaphors and stories he creates a picture that helps his players almost reach out and touch the concepts. *It is important to use examples that are relevant to your listener. Consequently, I use examples that are within the frame of reference of our players. It is*

very helpful if you can reinforce a point by saying, "You remember when."
If the example is something that they can personally remember, this imme-
diately creates a vivid frame of reference, so that there is that instant rela-
tionship — yes, they can get that picture of it in their mind. For example,
if in 1998, I gave them an example that took place in 1989, in their mind
they are saying, "1989 — wow, I was 9 years old then. What does this have
to do with me?" Therefore events that occurred before these youngsters
got here may be important, and occasionally be the subject of an example,
however, it is also important that I draw from situations that have taken
place in their tenure here. This allows them to have a better picture of
it.

These tangible images that Coach Snyder creates make a lasting
impression on his players and continue to motivate them long after they
leave the program. Chris Cobb describes how Coach Snyder "creates
things that we can see in order to emphasize a theoretical concept. The
'CatPack' is a good example of this. The 'CatPack' symbolizes 'There are
no individuals bigger than the team.'" Tom Byers, high school teacher and
football coach reinforces the power of the CatPack symbol.

> It is the little things that matter. A simple concept, but watch
> how the team takes the field and leaves the field holding hands.
> This is a physical reminder to us all that there are no individu-
> als. We are always a team. My fondest memory is having been
> part of something that has evolved over ten years. I think the
> bowl victory was nice but it was the five year journey from my
> redshirt freshman year, to the Copper Bowl victory in my senior
> year that I will always remember.

Sean Snyder looks to Coach Snyder as a "great teacher." "He can
always figure out an easier way for the players to understand what he
expects of them. He finds little techniques that help the players understand
the point he is trying to make." Coach Kramer describes how sometimes
what is seen or observed can make a point in ways that words can't.
"When we were working together at Austin College in the 70's one or two
players were not paying attention in a meeting. Bill got up, left the room,
and went to his office. Finally, one of the players went to get him and Bill
said, 'You are not serious or motivated. When you decide you are, let me
know and I will meet with you.' He had no problems after that."

Theoretical Context

Author Max DePree states that having a sound leadership philosophy is not enough — the leader must "connect tone and touch in communication." DePree further believes that behavior is the best way to communicate, whenever feasible. The lessons discussed in this chapter identify three specific strengths of Coach Snyder that have applicability for many of us. Snyder lets his behavior communicate his ideas, whenever possible, and he anchors or underscores his verbal messages with a tone and often a touch (particularly with his players) that communicates authenticity and sincerity. He will often touch your shoulder or your arm and look into your eyes while he talks softly to you. When this occurs, there is no question that you have his attention.

A second noteworthy communication strength is the ability to inspire. Transformational leadership is often linked in the literature with charisma. Because we believe the concept of charisma is often used in a stereotypical way, and has come to refer to superficial popularity, we prefer to substitute the term "inspirational." Inspiration is communication that provides enthusiasm and maintains momentum. Coach Snyder has demonstrated the remarkable ability to sustain this inspiration over a ten-year period. We believe that the ability to inspire others can be developed in everyone.

And lastly, Coach Snyder is a skilled and reflective listener. He listens intently, asks clarifying questions, and retains information. He is not concerned about stating his point of view until he is clear about what the other person is saying. He sincerely "seeks to understand, rather than to be understood."

For further information about leadership communication we recommend:

Armstrong, D.M. (1992). *Managing by Storying Around: A New Method of Leadership*. New York: Doubleday.

DePree, M. (1992). *Leadership Jazz*. New York: Doubleday.

Kouzes, J.M., and Posner, B.Z. (1987). *The Leadership Challenge: How to Get Extraordinary Things Done in Organizations*. San Francisco: Jossey-Bass.

Senge, P.M. (1990). *The Fifth Discipline*. New York: Doubleday.

Tannen, D.(1990). *You Just Don't Understand*. New York: Ballantine Books.

Chapter Four

Community

C HAPTER FOUR highlights the concept that successful organizations define and defend the notion of community. "Teamwork" is a hallmark of Coach Snyder's model of leadership. The next two Leadership Lessons address the issues of developing respect and organizational support.

Lesson Fourteen discusses the importance of defining an organization as consisting of all members holding equal importance.

Lesson Fifteen discusses the belief that demonstrating care to all members of an organization and its extended "family" is essential.

Leadership Lesson Number Fourteen

A sense of family is important in the organization. Each individual and every task should be valued by every member of the organization.

When Coach Snyder speaks of the football family, he is referring to everyone in the program; it is an inclusive term. For him "family" connotes a sense of caring and loyalty extended to everyone connected with the program. *We use the term "we" a lot. When we use "we," it means everybody. To put a successful organization together, you have to have a lot of people that are good at what they do, and who buy into a common vision and a common plan. In order for us to reach our goals we all have to be working together and pulling in the same direction. Every person in our program has a specific responsibility, a specific job to do. So it is not a casual decision to talk about the football family.*

In athletics, just as in any other organization, there are levels of responsibility, and each individual has specific responsibilities. Of course, everyone has ego needs that must be met. However, ego needs have the potential to harm an organization. We have all seen too many situations where ego conflicts have damaged the working environment, and pulled an organization in the wrong direction. Therefore, one of the foundation goals of our program is "Unity." For us, this means a coming together. I think a team approach is critical in a competitive environment, whether it be athletics, or anything else. The leader, whether head coach or CEO, must be an integral part of that team approach.

One of the first things that a visitor notices when entering the Vanier Complex is a sign that reads "Please wipe your feet." This is an example of Snyder's concept of valuing everyone's work and enhancing everyone's self respect. This sign is symbolic of the sense of family that he tries to create. When asked about the sign, he said, *That sign is not meant just for our players, but for everyone that enters this building. This sign is based on one of our most important premises. That premise is: "that we have people here who maintain our home." They are hard working roll-up-your-*

sleeves type of people — probably underpaid — who have pride in what they do.

Snyder wants the youngsters in the program to feel that they have a home on campus. *This is not a football factory. There are other positive things that take place in this building. We foster an attitude of wanting to help each other out. We are a team. Building supervisor Lyle Hasenbank and our maintenance staff are part of this team. And when I say "we," I include those people because they play a big role in what happens in the program.*

Some people tease me because in the winter, if I see muddy tracks come down the hall, I'll follow the tracks and I'm going to find the culprit. The culprit is normally someone not associated with the program, and usually an adult who would probably not do it in their own home. Our players know that when they leave the practice field they take their shoes off before they enter the building. They have learned not to put their responsibility on somebody else. It's that teamwork thing that says, "If I just do my little part, if I just take my shoes off and knock the dirt off of them, and take them in and put them in my locker, it is going to be less work for our custodian." It's just that simple.

Former quarterback Stan Weber confirms Coach Snyder's respect for everyone in the program. "Snyder does not diminish anyone. He knows the names of every person associated with the program and he knows what they do. One of the ways that he demonstrates that he values each job is that he holds everyone to the same standards of excellence as he does his star players."

Lyle Hasenbank confirms this point. "One of the things that I really admire about Coach Snyder is that my position is as important as the next one to him. I really appreciate that. It really does help when you know that he notices our work and asks others to have consideration for what we do."

The result of Coach Snyder's commitment to creating a family is that all family members become committed to the goals of the organization. Joan Friederich is a perfect example of the beneficial consequences of the family concept. She sincerely cares about the student-athletes in the program. "These kids are not just numbers down there on the field. They have faces, and names, and families. They are like my kids. Most of the people who leave here have learned discipline and respect. I was just talking to a player who graduated a few years ago and he said, 'You know when I was here I used to gripe about everything, but boy I really miss it. I really appreciate now what we did then.'" Friederich believes that,

> By demanding so much from his players, Coach Snyder is preparing them for the real world, where it is not easy either. I get tears in my eyes when I think of how proud I am of our team, and players, and fans. You don't have to spend too much time around him to see that he cares deeply about the youth of our society, not just the players on his team. I think Coach is on a mission to help the youth of the country. When he speaks he does not talk about football, he talks about helping kids. He really cares about the youth of America. He spends a lot of time with parents when they come with their sons for their campus visits. He will take as much time as they need. He is so consistent in what he does. Even in the office when someone upsets him he never embarrasses them; he never humiliates anyone. If he has to reprimand someone he does it in private. When we have a staff party it includes everyone from the maintenance crew to the President of the University.

Be Sure That Your Actions Honor Your Priorities

Coach Snyder's commitment to the youth of the community was recently highlighted in a newspaper article written by Carrie Miller. Writing for the *Manhattan Mercury*, she reported on a once-a-year event called "lay person Sunday." On this day, a church member is invited to give the sermon. This year Coach Snyder delivered a message entitled *Guiding, Leading and Directing the Youth of a Troubled Society.* Snyder based his talk on Proverbs 22:6, "Train up a child in the way he should go and when he is old he will not depart from it." There is not a better one-sentence description of the mission of Coach Snyder's life. "During his talk, he urged his listeners to take any opportunity they have to counsel young people and help them through "the tremendous pressures they face."

Coach Snyder's commitment to a sense of family, respect for every task, and the "we" philosophy is noticed by his colleagues and other professionals. Stan Weber believes that Snyder's consistent reinforcement of the idea that everyone is of equal value to the football program has a positive carryover to the way people in the program relate and behave toward others outside of the program. Weber remarks, "Being a family is a critical key that stimulates his players to be leaders and treat others equally."

Others outside of the program notice the impact of the family commitment. Businessman Dennis Mullin states,

> Coach makes it clear to everyone that no one individual can be a success, without the help of many others. In this day and age you see so many people that are always looking out for "number one." Coach is the best example that I have ever seen of the concept that, "I can't do anything, but we can do everything."
>
> When Coach Snyder looks at a high school student, he sees a potential success story in life. The people in the program understand what he is doing. However, it's the fans that sometimes lose sight of his goals. I think that is one of the reasons that he spends time speaking to service groups, so that we enthusiastic fans can understand the bigger picture.

Mullin explains another example of Coach Snyder's commitment to the total student.

> Each year a function is held in Kansas City that gives seniors the opportunity to meet the business world and tell us about themselves. One aspect of the family nature of the team is that in many cases Bill must act like a father to them. Like all fathers, he is sometimes loved and is sometimes hated because he teaches them responsibility. He teaches them discipline. He teaches them some of the qualities that will help them succeed in life. But I will guarantee you that he will have a tremendous percentage of his student athletes that look back and see Bill Snyder as one of the reasons for their success.

> **?**
>
> As the KSU football team continues to get better, the players become role models for the university and the community. How do you help them develop such leadership skills as public speaking and motivational skills?
>
> Verneta White
Class of '99, Kansas City, Kansas
>
> *By placing them into those roles in our program. Players are called upon to address their teammates about intrinsic values, appropriate behavior and team goals and objectives. Our staff frequently addresses our team about these same values and the traits of quality leadership and role modeling. Players are then placed into community, school, and youth programs addressing and counseling young people.*
>
> *Coach Snyder*

Coach Snyder is very aware of the potential for misunderstanding as he attempts to assist his players' development into the best people that they can be. *I probably come across like I want to control the lives of those in our program. This actually is not my intent. I don't want to, and I know that I can't control what they do away from the program. What I ask is for everyone in the program to respect each other and to respect confidences shared within the family. Everyone in the family has a responsibility to understand and accept responsibility for their actions. Coaches and assistant coaches are very similar to anyone in management. I am responsible for my assistant coaches and they are responsible for the actions of the players that they coach. My assistants understand that I hold them responsible for the players that they work with. They are responsible for a variety of different things outside the scope of athletics. This is certainly another way that athletics is not a perfect metaphor for other workplaces. I doubt that a manager at Ford Motor Company is put in a position to accept responsibility for what happens to John Q. Worker after work.*

I have always believed that coaches should be held responsible for the actions of their players, day or night. The total life of the student-athlete is important to me, and is something that I have some responsibility for. As coaches, we need to accept this role, because we are talking about young people engaged in college football. None of us must ever lose sight of the fact that this is an educational institution. As hard as it may be for some people to believe, the education of the players is the most important facet of what we are trying accomplish. In addition to the lessons they learn in their classrooms, they are learning many important lessons in the football program. In order for this to happen, coaches have some responsibility for what their players do off the football field. I am not capable of supervising one hundred and twenty youngsters, but I have nine coaches who can share in that responsibility, and they are accountable.

This concept of family and loyalty has had a big impact on his players. Chris Cobb remembers that,

> Before Coach Snyder arrived at Kansas State, walk-ons were treated like dirt, treated like meat. They had different locker rooms, and they ate at different places. Coach Snyder has always been committed to giving several walk-on scholarships. One of the first things he did was have the wall that separated the two locker rooms knocked down. He also made sure that everyone ate together. He treated everybody like a winner. He treated everyone like they were an integral part of the team. We became a fellowship of guys united for one goal. It was very clear that the rules he made were for everyone.

Cobb continues,

> One of the sixteen goals for success was to treat everybody equal, respect each other. Each of us was like a spoke on a wheel. Without one, the wheel would be out of round, and would not run smoothly. If you have a team where some players think they are worth more than other players, your wheel will not spin smoothly. When he first came some of his ideas seemed like a bunch of hogwash to a group of eighteen, nineteen, twenty, or twenty-one-year-old students. It took him all of that first spring and five or six games into our first season to get it ingrained into our heads that we were not a bunch of individuals. Eventually, we began to absorb what he was doing.

Matt Miller has had the opportunity to participate in the program as a player and now as a graduate assistant. "Some of the guys that come into the program have had a pretty tough life. It is really neat watching those guys transform from distrustful individuals to part of a family. After a short time, no one wants to let their brothers down."

For many players, Coach Snyder is almost like a father, especially for those who are a long way from home. Kevin Lockett talks to Coach Snyder about once a month. "He is a very positive person and has been a very positive role model for me. He always has the right thing to say."

The sense of family does not end when a player leaves the program. Former player Mark Porter, who finished his eligibility before Coach Snyder arrived at Kansas State, commented that "Coach Snyder has really been supportive of me. I wanted to go pro and he allowed me to use the facilities anytime I wanted. I tried for four or five years to go into the NFL. He not only allowed me to continue to use the facilities, he was always very encouraging."

A critical part of the process of developing a family environment is the Big Brother program. Mike "Crash" Ekeler believes that this program

> Made a real difference. It places a senior with a freshman and it makes everyone look at the team as a second family. He preaches that all the time, "family, family, family." It does not matter if you are black or white. We are all in the same boat. We all practice together and have one common goal. This draws the one hundred and twenty guys together. One of the hardest things about graduating is that you are losing that family. I know that there was not one person there that would not help me if I ever needed help.

Leadership Lesson Number Fifteen

Sincere interest and concern must be regularly demonstrated to each member of the organization.

Demonstrating sincere concern to both current and past players and members and their families is a hallmark of Coach Snyder's leadership. However, during the process of interviewing him for this book, we found it impossible to draw him into any discussion about his good works. In fact, he shies away from any conversation that might lead to the misconception that he is interested in self aggrandizement. Hence, in order to expand on the importance of a leader demonstrating that he or she cares, we will draw on our personal observations of him, and the observations of others.

Each year when Snyder addresses his coaching staff at the beginning of the season, he reminds them that, *It is important for our players to know that we care about them. It is equally important that we demand a great deal of them and that we hold them accountable for their performance both on and off the field. To do both is not an easy task and must be well thought out and well planned. There is a fine line between showing a player you are for him and still being able to demand great performance without letting him do less than he is capable of. Communication is the vital factor. Your players must be told what you expect, why you expect it, and what the consequences are. They must be told how you will respond and what that means. Yelling, screaming and swearing is not the answer. You can be very demanding without that. Accepting mistakes and less than a player's best performance is also not the answer. He must know that you will not tolerate less than his best, yet he must know that you love him like your own. This is the true art of coaching.*

If you visualize concentric circles radiating out from Coach Snyder you will have an idea of how he demonstrates his interest and concern. In the circle that is closest to him is his family. The three things that are most important to him are his family, his faith and football. Sean Snyder observes that, "He likes to brighten the eyes of a youngster. It is just like my kids. When they come up and run down the hall and bang on the door, he stops what he is doing, brings them into his office, gives them a piece of candy, and spends time talking with them. I see an ease that comes over him whenever he is able to make a kid laugh or make kid smile." Tim Fitzgerald, editor and publisher of *Powercat Illustrated,* says,

> It is clear to those who are around him that Coach Snyder is committed to his family. You often hear stories of his flying back from a game and playing with his youngest daughter on the plane. Every moment has a purpose, and can be used. Everything he does is focused on his family or on the football program. Accordingly, watching the final episode of *Seinfeld* or reading a novel does not move him forward in either of these areas. He has no hobbies, because he does not need a distraction from anything. The two things he loves the most, the two things that he derives the greatest pleasure and enjoyment from are family and football. He pours himself into those two things.

His players are in the next circle outside of his family. Women's basketball coach Deb Patterson is in a unique position to comment on Coach Snyder's concern for his players. She believes that communicating and sharing with people that they are valued and needed in the program is very important. "I think, to a large extent, organizations succeed to a level commensurate with the level to which the people in the organization feel needed, respected, appreciated, and guided."

Stan Weber shares the belief that demonstrating sincere concern is a critical factor in organizational success.

> Coach Snyder goes around to the people in his program and looks them in the eye and communicates with them. This does not mean that every interaction must be intense or a high level interaction. But by taking the time to spend a few minutes in conversation demonstrates that you care enough to look them in the eye and talk to them. Each player knows that Coach Snyder recognizes him as an individual. Each knows that Coach Snyder may be watching him while he is practicing. This player's goal may not be to be named an All-American, it may be to demonstrate to Coach Snyder that he is improving.

Stan Weber notes that before each game, "Coach Snyder goes around and shakes hands with every player. He does it because it matters to those players, but it doesn't hurt that the parents see their son being treated the right way. When you do the right things for the right reason you will get additional benefits. It is pretty impressive to hear writers up in the press box say, "You know if I had a kid who was a great athlete, I would want him to play for Bill Snyder.'"

Other professionals confirm Snyder's sincere interest in others both inside and outside the program. Max Urick coached with Woody Hays at Ohio State, and has had the opportunity to observe coaches for over 30 years. According to Urick, "Coach Snyder doesn't just talk about caring, he demonstrates it on a daily basis. People know that Coach Snyder spends a lot of time working. What most people don't see is how much of that time is spent talking with his players. The most important thing you could give an athlete is your time. Coach Snyder meets with his players a lot. He meets with them as a group and he meets with them individually."

Parents of players also confirm the importance of demonstrated care to family members. One parent told us that her son has a learning disability. Coach Snyder told the youngster that, "'We really would like to have you on our team. We will wait until you get eligible.' He didn't have to do that. Because of Coach Snyder's encouragement our son played for four years and got a scholarship for his fifth year. He graduated. This wouldn't have happened at some of the other schools that were recruiting him. Yes, Coach Snyder is a task master, but I find him to have a lot of compassion."

Sandy Beisel, another parent, comments, "What I've seen from the outside, looking in, is that Coach Snyder and his staff are very concerned about the families of the players, not just the player. He always personally welcomes parents when they come to a game and makes us feel at home."

Most importantly, the players themselves shared numerous examples of Coach Snyder's sincere concern. Matt Miller recalls that Coach Snyder is,

> . . . Constantly asking team captains how the players are feeling. He's always wanting to make things better for students on the field, in the classroom, and as people. He really uses his team captains to help him know if there's anything wrong or any way that he can help. I noticed this when I was a player, but as

an assistant I see it from another perspective. He is always asking us if we have talked to so and so. He also has us check on players that were here six or seven years ago and need 12 hours to graduate.

Some cynics may think Coach Snyder is only concerned about these people because they think that it helps Kansas State's graduation rate for athletes. However, the NCAA only credits people who graduate within five years of enrollment.

Each player we talked to had a personal story that demonstrated the impact of Coach Snyder's personal attention on their lives after football. Former defensive end John Butler remembers:

> He always instilled how important it was to be polite all of the time. And you know, I have found that being polite can get you a long way in this world. I have found in my current job that when you are cordial and personable to people they will usually respond the same way. You know he always took the time to send each player a personal birthday note. I don't know why I remember this, but it just shows how he takes the time to do the little things that make you feel like an individual.
>
> Coach Snyder knows everybody's name, not just the names of the great players like Andre Coleman, but he knew the name of the freshman walk on from a small rural town in western Kansas who did not get a scholarship, and he knew my name. He would walk up to us and ask us how the dorms were, or if we were getting enough to eat. He could look in your eyes and ask you how your parents were doing, and you knew he really was interested.

Tom Byers, a former free-safety who is now a teacher and football coach, recalls,

> Coach Snyder was always looking out for the team. After our victory over Kansas in 1991, Governor Joan Finney invited the team to the governor's mansion for dinner. Coach Snyder told us not to eat anything before we got there, because there would be plenty of food. We packed the whole team into the mansion,

it was pretty jam packed with a hundred and twenty big football players. About halfway through the serving line they ran out of food. The guys at the end of the line did not get much to eat. On the way back we were moaning and groaning about how hungry we were. When we got back to the complex the coach told us to go to the Big Eight Room. When we got there, there was a whole pizza for each of us. He is always looking out for us. It might be something big or a subtle thing, but it really makes a difference.

Although some of the stories are humorous, others are more serious. Kitt Rawlings, assistant coach at Southwest Missouri State, remembers something that happened in 1992.

We had a running back, Eric Gallon, who was a great athlete and a real team leader. Football was everything to Eric, he had hopes of playing professionally. During spring drills he hurt his knee and needed total reconstruction surgery. When Eric got hurt, Coach Snyder caught up with him as he was being taken off the field. The coach wanted to make sure Eric had things in proper perspective. During Eric's rehabilitation Coach Snyder would not let him get depressed. He helped Eric develop a very specific plan to help him get back on the field and do what he really loved to do. Eric went on to have a great year, and set some records. This is not an isolated example. Watch him during a game. You will see his sincere concern for his players during the games. With all the things he has to think about in a game, when a player gets hurt, he could send someone else to check him out, and go on with the game plan, but he always goes out to his player to see how he is. He does it regardless of whether the player is on the first team or the fifth team.

This interest in his players does not end when they graduate. Laird Veatch recalls, "When I was done playing he was really helpful. He got me off on the right foot, and pointed me in the right direction. I know that if I ever needed him, he would be there for me." Matt Garber gives Coach Snyder a lot of credit for his career success.

When I was just deciding to get into coaching, I talked to him a lot about how he did some of the things that he did. He likes to check up on his players and he likes to hear that we are doing good things. He is not just focused on football, he is pretty personable. He is sincerely interested in our lives even after we leave his program. I know that many of his former players stop by his office whenever we are back to Manhattan.

NFL player Kevin Lockett speaks of how important Coach Snyder's attitude is, especially for players who are far from home.

After a week of being away from home, I was not even playing on the redshirt freshmen team, and he called me into his office. This was the first of several instances through my career that he would call me into the office and talk to me about things that had nothing to do with football. He wanted to know how my family was, how things were going personally, how school was going. He wanted to know how I was making the transition from high school to college. He always asked what he could do to help. He gets a lot of freshmen through that first year. It is very difficult to leave your home and go to college, where you really don't know a lot of people and you are on your own. It was just this kind of thing that he and the other coaches would do to really help you feel that you were fitting in and he really wanted you to be there.

According to Matt Garber,

He cares about us as players, but he really cares about us as individuals. One thing that really impressed me was something that he did after I graduated. One of my nephews had been diagnosed with leukemia. He loved to go to football games, but he was on medication and he could not be around people. I don't know how Coach Snyder found out about it, I did not tell him. But, he contacted my brother-in-law, and asked how it was going, and if he could help with anything. He offered to help my nephew get to the game. He worked it all out for my nephew. It was the KU football game, a very big day. This is just one example of Coach Snyder's continued efforts to help. Something that really was special that few people know about.

Theoretical Context

Each of us who aspire to be leaders can benefit from this lesson. Taking the time to demonstrate your concern for your peers and your subordinates will have an impact on your success as a leader.

DuBrin, quoting Evereed and Selman, states that coaching as a leadership philosophy is a "paradigm shift from traditional management, which focuses heavily on control, order and compliance." Coaching as a leadership philosophy provides an excellent structure for developing the needed sense of community. They list the following defining traits of the coaching/leadership model:

- a good coach is more concerned about developing members of his or her team than controlling them;

- coaching is a dyad that cannot exist without interaction between at least two participants; and

- coaching requires a high degree of interpersonal risk and trust on the part of the participants.

Coach Snyder obviously exemplifies the above traits. However, he extends the notion of community to include the family of the team and staff, as well as former staff and team members. He understands that no member of his team lives in a vacuum. Each participant is connected to others outside of the program. Imagine how the enthusiasm and motivation of members of any organization would increase if all leaders recognized and attended to a broader definition of a sense of community.

For further information about community we recommend:

Chrislip, D., and Larson, C. (1994). *Collaborative Leadership: How Citizens and Civic Leaders Can Make a Difference.* San Francisco: Jossey-Bass.

DuBrin, A. J. (1998). *Leadership Research Findings, Practice, and Skills.* Boston: Houghton Mifflin Co.

Greenleaf, R. K., Frick, D. M., and Spears, L. C. (1996). *On Becoming a Servant Leader*. San Francisco: Jossey-Bass.

Kelley, R. E. (1992). *The Power of Followership*. New York: Doubleday.

Chapter Five

Credibility

C HAPTER FIVE examines the concept of credibility and how Coach Snyder establishes and maintains credibility. This chapter includes three Leadership Lessons that address the issues of credibility, the importance of consistency, and specific methods for developing credibility.

Lesson Sixteen describes attributes of credibility.

Lesson Seventeen discusses the role that time plays in earning credibility.

Lesson Eighteen presents specific methods of establishing credibility.

Leadership Lesson Number Sixteen

Integrity, honesty, and trustworthiness are the leader's most important attributes.

The K-State football program has avoided many of the ethical problems that regularly beset major college football programs. Coach Snyder's personal integrity, and his reinforcement of doing the right thing for the right reasons, is a significant factor in the high standards of citizenship held by most of his team. The student athletes at Kansas State attempt to emulate Coach Snyder's behaviors because they trust his judgment. People who have worked with him are absolutely confident that he has the highest standards of integrity. He is a credible leader. This credibility was demonstrated early in his loyalty to the University of Iowa. After accepting the position at Kansas State University he informed K-State that he planned on working Iowa's bowl game and would continue to make those preparations. He told them, "I am a strong believer in loyalty, and I have that loyalty to the Iowa coaching staff and to the players of Iowa."

As with several other lessons, Coach Snyder does not talk about himself. In order to evaluate this lesson in terms of its consequences, we will depend on the words of others. For example, Deb Patterson agrees that character education is part of coaching. "Coach Snyder and I both talk about values, morals, and ethics. Value leadership means talking about the character of people first." As faculty representative to the conference and the NCAA, Bob Snell has had an opportunity to scrutinize Coach Snyder's behavior in a unique way. He states that, "There's never been any question in my mind about him wanting to do the right thing. There is no question that he will not cheat, nor will he tolerate anyone else cheating." Provost Jim Coffman refers to Coach Snyder as "a class act."

I closely watch the ethics of people representing Kansas State. My perception is that he treats everyone fairly and with respect. For me, the proof is in the pudding. Indications that he practices what he preaches can be seen in the fact that coaches and players are not fighting with each other; his players say the same thing that Bill says in public; and he has been here too long to have been able to carry off a hoax. If he wasn't the real thing, if he was just throwing up smoke, it would have been seen by somebody by now.

Dennis Mullin observes that Coach Snyder is, "highly ethical, . . . bar none. Honesty is just a way of life for him. For Coach, honesty and concern are not public relations ploys. Coach is always going to do what he believes is right for the individual."

The trait that stands out for Wichita businessman Howard Sherwood is Coach Snyder's character. "It's above reproach. I just can't imagine an issue or anybody saying anything negative about him or questioning his character. In this day and age in athletics, that is a little unique. Character has kind of taken a back seat in a lot of success stories, but not his."

In 1997 the Air Force ROTC unit named Coach Snyder the Honorary Detachment Commander. According to Major Steve Dorfman,

The most important factor that we look at when selecting a person for this honor is the fact that he walks the talk of what we tell our cadets. He is our core values, integrity first, excellence in all you do and service before self. We expect our cadets to look at integrity first.

He lives the same standard that he sets for others. He doesn't lie. He doesn't tolerate lying. He expects everybody to play fair with him, and he'll play fair with them in return. There is excellence in all he does. I mean, he gives his team and the football program one hundred percent and in return he expects everyone associated with the football program to give him one hundred percent. That's something that we also look at. And the other thing that we look at is service before self. We tell our students, you're not a pilot, you're not a navigator, you're not a support person. You're an officer first. Well, Coach Snyder does the same thing. The player's job is to play football, not when they feel like it and not halfheartedly. You play football. Your primary job here, besides getting an education, which he stresses very heavily, and which I like to see, is to play football for K-State.

Quentin Neujahr vividly explains how Coach Snyder's integrity is put into practice. "Occasionally a player will get into some type of trouble. When this has happened Coach Snyder always says the same thing, 'I will do as much as I can to help you, within the limits of the law. But I am not going to bend or break the law for you. I won't do that for anybody. Each of you needs to understand that you must abide by the law just like everybody else.'"

?

What do you do when you make a mistake?
What do you do when someone who works for you makes a mistake?
What do you do when someone who thinks they are working in your best interest makes a mistake?

Amy Donahy
Class of '98, Paola, Kansas

Correct it.
Help them correct it.
Help them correct it.

Coach Snyder

Coach Snyder does the right thing, for the right reason, and in the right way. The impact of Snyder's example can be seen in the following excerpts from a recent letter to the *Manhattan Mercury* written by Barry A. Clark, a Manhattan resident.

To the Editor:
Several days ago I had the privilege of meeting a remarkable K-State football player under circumstances that should be brought to your attention. On May 4, I was preparing to leave Manhattan for a fishing trip to Colorado. I normally don't carry much cash, but on this occasion I withdrew $150 for miscellaneous travel expenses and was carrying the money in a clip in my pocket, when I noticed the money clip was missing. I dropped by the store in Aggieville where I had fueled my car. . . . The clerk told me that a man had found the clip and provided me with a note bearing a telephone number and with

"Chris, leave message" written upon it. I returned home, called the number and waited for a response. Two hours later, a young man called. He explained that he had found my money clip on the ground, but his conscience would not allow him to keep it. . . . He invited me over (after asking me to describe the money clip) at which time I packed up my little boy and proceeded to the home of Chris Claybon. Chris and his roommates were grilling hot dogs; not only did I recover my clip and all the money, but my boy and I got dinner in the process.

Chris Claybon has shown that he is a young man with true character. What better test than to do the right thing when one could do the wrong thing with absolutely no chance of being discovered. Through his actions, Chris had demonstrated his integrity, while serving as a tremendous example to others.

Leadership Lesson Number Seventeen

Credibility is earned and established over time.

When we asked Coach Snyder to talk about the concept of credibility, he made it clear that he did not think a person can plan or scheme to be credible. *I think credibility is in the eyes of the beholder. I am honored to learn that people think of me in that way because I would like to be understood as being credible, accountable, trustworthy. Those are important traits to have if you are going to be in a leadership position. The worst thing in the world is to have a leader that you cannot trust. I know that I don't function well in an arena where there is a lack of trust. A lack of trust causes you to be too guarded, and always having to be guarded is time consuming. I don't think our program could be successful if people within this program didn't attach credibility to what I do and what I say. Trust is very important in motivation. Football programs as well as corporations need to be able to motivate their people.*

Credibility is doing what you say you are going to do, earning trust over time, listening to and responding to others' issues, and sharing accolades with others, while taking responsibility for any failures.

When we asked him to tell us what credibility means to him and to give us some examples of who he believes is credible, he responded by saying, *Before someone has credibility with me I need to understand that individual fairly well. For example, I couldn't tell you whether Harry Truman was credible, because I didn't know Harry Truman. Credibility means you can trust someone, to bank your life on someone. Most of the people who have credibility with me are people I am with on a very regular basis. For example, my wife and children are credible, my coaches are credible, my secretary Joan is credible, the athletic director, Max Urick, is credible, Vice-president Bob Krause is credible, President Jon Wefald is credible. Credibility means that I can count on them. Credibility is important to me. A credible person is accountable and trustworthy.*

There aren't many athletes that can jump on a field and find success in a unit or a team without being highly motivated. Sometimes individuals, for a variety of reasons, don't have the capacity to create that motivation within themselves. Therefore, someone has to inspire that motivation. No one is going to be inspired by someone they have no trust in or who is not credible. It's important, in our program, that there is a trust not just of Bill Snyder, but a trust of each other in the program. This is a very big thing. Each player must be able to line up on Saturday afternoon and have trust in the guy that is right there next to them. When it gets down to the last play of the ball game, and it's a difference between a win and a loss, each player must have absolute confidence that every other player is going to give it everything he's got. And each player has to be accountable enough that every other player trusts him to do exactly the same thing. The success of the football team is built on trust and credibility.

Many people seem to want a "quick fix." These people want to step into a classroom, or an office, or a factory — or step into whatever their leadership role is — and immediately have credibility. Everyone wishes they could just say, "Listen, you can trust me," and they would be trusted. I don't think it happens this way. It takes time to earn people's trust. The solution is to do what you say you're going to do, be yourself, be genuine, care about the people that you are involved with, make them important to you. Do things that show them that you have an interest in them, take time for them, spend time with them, show that you have some interest in things other than just what is on your job responsibilities. Demonstrate that you have an interest in their family, that you care about their children, that you understand that they have child care problems, or have insurance problems, or if they have benefits problems. Demonstrate that you are willing to listen to what they have to say and that you will do the best to help them find solutions.

You can encourage them to bring their problems to you, but it's not a matter of them bringing problems to you. You must also go to them and say, "What are the problems in our organization?" I think what used to be called "brainstorming sessions" are good. I think it's good to go in front of your people once in a while and say, "How's this area?" or "Let's talk about this," or throw ideas out for discussion. You need to listen to them, and not just talk at them. Saying that you want to hear what they are thinking, and then not listening is the quickest way to lose credibility. If you do this you will be worse off than if you never asked.

Leaders Must Do What They Say They Are Going to Do

The bottom line is this, if you do what you say you're going to do, even if you say I'm going to fire you if you don't get the job done, then you have got to follow up. You better be prepared to fire them. There's credibility in that. I don't want to play games. I don't want to try to play cat and mouse. You need to clearly communicate your expectations and then hold people accountable for their actions. It's really about communication. When there is a problem with performance, I sit down with the person and say, "This isn't being done the way it should be done. You need to get it done this way. I'm going to give you an opportunity to do it again. Is there a reason you can't do it this particular way and give us a better finished product? If there is a reason, then tell me what that reason is and I will help try to find a way to dissolve that reason." I understand that everybody can't do everything. We need to make sure that that every particular thing is accomplished the way it should be. I have a pretty straight forward approach to problem solving.

It's important to me that our players understand that when there is something that has been negative, when we didn't do as we should have in terms of our own preparation, then that falls in the lap of Coach Snyder. They need to understand that when we're successful I'm going to get more accolades than I want. That is not where the praise should go. I wish that the accolades would be distributed to all those who deserve them. But it is important for the players to understand that I identify myself, or any of our coaches, when we make some errors in judgment, referring to the ball game and our preparation. The players understand that we make some mistakes and take the consequences for those mistakes. They also see that we take immediate steps to correct those mistakes that we make.

Because Coach Snyder has credibility, stereotypes about football players and football coaches are beginning to crumble at Kansas State University. Provost Jim Coffman cites the following example:

> We were planning a department heads retreat in January of 1997. The focus of the retreat was to talk about reworking the university's curriculum. Several department heads joined my staff to plan the retreat. One of the department heads said, "There is someone on this campus who could help us with this retreat. He has successfully totally revised his program from top to bottom. This person is Bill Snyder." Upon reflection I agreed.

Consequently, I invited Coach Snyder to be the luncheon speaker for the retreat.

I quickly learned that this decision did not sit very well with a few of the department heads. They told me that they did not need a motivational speaker. They said that they preferred someone talking about substantive issues. But let me tell you — Bill Snyder's speech had substance. His strategic, value based goal setting and his philosophy of getting better every day had real applicability for the department heads. I even heard from one of the people who had originally complained. He said he had been wrong and he had learned quite a bit from Coach Snyder.

Credibility is hard earned, but essential to effective leadership. Credibility means that you tell the truth, even if it would be easier to avoid it. In the long run integrity pays off in big dividends. Pat Scott, coach and middle school teacher in Victoria, Kansas, states, "A former player of mine, who now plays for K-State, told me how impressed he was with Coach Snyder's honesty. The player said that coaches at other schools had guaranteed him that he would start as a freshman. However, K-State was very up front, genuine, honest. They told him, "You are going to have to earn your spot."

When students do not respect a teacher or a coach they make their feelings known. Mordean Taylor-Archer is in a position to talk with many athletes. She notes, "The players hold him in high-esteem and he has their respect. They feel that they can talk and share things with him, and at the same time, they understand that he's going to make the calls."

Over the years, Lawrence business person Steve Johnson has listened to Snyder speak many times. He recalls that, "Coach Snyder is always impressive because he very seldom wants to talk about x's and o's or scores or people's success on the football field, or who is planning to come to Kansas State. He always talks about the success of the players individually. He talks about whether they're going to be good students and good people and make a success of themselves in their lives. He talks from the heart every time, and he always talks about the kids and the success of the kids."

According to Jim Epps, Coach Snyder has been credible from the beginning, and Snyder also insists that others view K-State as credible.

An event that demonstrates Coach Snyder's credibility, courage, and seriousness occurred right after he accepted the position. We did a barnstorming tour around the state to all of the Catbacker groups. This meeting took place at a large sports bar in Overland Park. Bill was introduced and got up on a chair, where the audience could see and hear him. He expressed his appreciation for the support and began to tell them about his objectives.

There were two guys close to me, and about five feet from Bill. They had been drinking and began to jeer and mock Bill. "We have heard all this BS before. You won't last any longer than the last ten coaches." After each of their comments they laughed loudly. Coach Snyder noticed them and made eye contact with them. As soon as he concluded his speech he stepped down and walked right up to these two fellows, and they were pretty big guys. He got right in their face, and in a very controlled, but unmistakable fashion, said, "I did not take this job to have people badger me and make fun of Kansas State's football program!"

He made it clear that he did not appreciate their behavior, and he was not going to put up with it. This incident demonstrated Bill's tremendous resolve. He was not going to let anyone make fun of his program.

John Butler puts it well by adding, "Coach Snyder said we would win. He said it would not be easy, and there would be disappointments, but if we did the hard work we would win. As I look back now, it is clear that to be a credible person you have to constantly demonstrate that you are honest and this has to take place over a period of time."

Leadership Lesson Number Eighteen

A standard of excellence can only be established and maintained by hard work and role modeling.

It is impossible to overestimate the value that Coach Snyder places on hard work — there is no substitute. As we mentioned in earlier chapters, hard work without a plan is wasted energy. However, the best designed plan will be ineffective if you do not exert significant effort. Snyder makes no apologies for demanding hard work and expecting excellence from everyone, all of the time. He acknowledges his rigorous standard and is not apologetic about it. However, Dennis Mullin is correct when he adds that Coach Snyder never asks anyone to work harder than he is going to work himself. Bob Krause observes that Coach Snyder is very fair with his players and staff. Krause paraphrases Snyder when he says, "I'm going to demand things out of you that have never been demanded of you before in your life. And if you do the work and make the commitment, good things will happen to you."

I would never want to say that my way is the right way or the only way or that you should do it like I do. It's just the way I do things. I wouldn't know what name to put with what I do. I do know that I make a lot of mistakes. However, I care about the people that are part of what we do. I care about our coaches and I care about the youngsters in the program. However, I'm a pretty demanding individual. The people who have been around me understand that. We use "demanding" in our terminology a great deal. There are just certain things that need to be demanded if you want to get the job done. And you can be demanding without necessarily being a harsh individual. My style is to simply demand that it be done. If you are going to succeed you have to complete the steps. We ask our people not to accept anything less than our very best.

Manhattan business leader Tracey DeBruyn refers to Coach Snyder as a person who believes in "doing the common thing, uncommonly well." Coach Snyder's high expectations impact all those around him. Greg Sharpe indicates that Coach Snyder "has taught me to set my sights a little higher than I might have two or three years ago. And in turn, I convey high expectations to those that I work with."

It is impressive to speak with Coach Snyder's former athletes and listen to them talk about the impact he had on them. For example, Kirby Hocutt remembers,

> The thing that has had the most impact on my life is the work ethic that you develop in the football program at Kansas State. It is not the easiest of times. There are a lot of pressures on you as you attempt to succeed as a football player and in the classroom. This is a huge burden, and it is one that only a certain number of individuals are willing to take on. What impressed me, and what convinced me to do the work was that come Saturday afternoon I knew that we were going to be competitive to play. And the reason that I knew that was, because of the work and preparation that was put in by Coach Snyder, the assistant coaches, and everyone within the program. Seeing how hard the coaches worked actually motivated us. We were willing to devote twenty hours of our week, because we knew that the coaches were putting in four times the effort and work that we were.

Quentin Neujahr remembers an incident that is typical of Coach Snyder's commitment to using every minute to the best advantage.

> One day we were practicing, and there was a tornado watch for all of Riley County. You could see the clouds coming in, and the players kept glancing at them. We started to lose our concentration. Coach Snyder blew his whistle. We thought practice was going to be called off; however, when Coach called us together he sent us to the indoor facility so we would not be distracted. We all knew that somewhere down the line it was going to pay off.

Who are a few people that you believe would be good role models for young people today?

> Casey Carlson
> Class of '97, '98, Solomon, Kansas

?

Mother Teresa, Michael Jordan, Bill Gates, Billy Graham, and Colin Powell would all serve as good role models.

> *Coach Snyder*

A Leader Must Teach By Example

Many former players carry the strong work ethic into their work lives. Danny Needham recalls, "He teaches by example how to manage people. If you pay attention, you can learn a lot about working with people by the way he interacts with his staff and players. I work in sales and my livelihood depends on how well I work with people. I use what he taught me every day. He has credibility because he always does what he says he will do."

Laird Veatch credits Coach Snyder with preparing him for the real world. "Once you have gone through the demands that are expected of you in the football program at Kansas State, through the two-a-days, the winter agilities, all the work, it really makes you realize that no matter what you are faced with later in life, you can handle it. There are things that come up in life that are tough for anybody. But if you have had that kind of background that we players have had, you can always lean on it and remember. He is always pushing us to get closer to each other, to rely on each other more. That prepares you for working with people the rest of your life. He teaches you not only how to get along with people, but how to be a leader. He does a great job of helping his players become leaders. One of the ways that he does this is by expecting a lot from the upperclassmen. By the time you are an upperclassman you know what it takes to be a leader. That stays with you for the rest of your life."

Theoretical Context

Of the six aspects of Coach Snyder's leadership that we have included in this book, we find the issue of credibility to be one of the most significant. James Kouzes and Barry Posner assert in their book, *Credibility,* that the most basic characteristic of any admired leader is his or her credibility.

After reviewing data over a ten-year period, they found that credibility is consistently defined as someone who is: honest, forward-looking, inspiring, and competent. Without exception, everyone that we interviewed confirmed our personal observation that Coach Snyder is the "real deal." He does not have the time nor an interest in pretending to be something or someone that he is not.

According to Kouzes and Posner, "If credibility is the foundation of leadership then our society is in trouble, as our leaders are not faring well on the credibility scale." The authors continue to say that we "have seen a large-scale erosion of employee confidence in management over the last decade." Additionally, they cite a study by Donald Kanter and Philip Mirvis which found that in the early 1990's, 48 percent of American workers were cynical about leaders. Anyone interested in leadership and motivating people to improve must be alarmed by this information.

Coach Snyder is not only honest, but he presents trustworthiness, hard work, role-modeling and a consistent standard of excellence as antidotes to society's cynicism. In his case, what you see is truly what you get. Many of the lessons presented in this book depend on the credibility of the leader. People are not going to work as hard, be as committed, be as loyal, or care as much if the leader is not credible.

For information about credibility we recommend:

Gardner, J. W. (1990). *On Leadership*. New York: Free Press.

Heifetz, R. A. (1994). *Leadership without Easy Answers*. Cambridge, MA: Belknap Press.

Kouzes, J. M., and Posner, B. Z. (1993). *Credibility: How Leaders Gain and Lose It, Why People Demand It*. San Francisco: Jossey-Bass.

Chapter Six

Day-To-Day Management

$\mathcal{T}$HE FINAL TWO LESSONS detail the importance of time and stress management as well as consistency and attention to detail. Coach Snyder and other leaders make use of the specific management methods explained in this chapter.

Lesson Nineteen documents the importance of consistency and attention to detail.

Lesson Twenty presents specific strategies to manage priorities, time, stress, and emotions.

Leadership Lesson Number Nineteen

Attention to detail and consistency are essential to transforming an organization's climate, and necessary for the continual improvement of the organization.

Coach Snyder's well-known focus on details has been demonstrated already in this book. In this section, Coach Snyder gives specific examples of how he translates the concept of attending to details to the reality of leading a football program.

I keep a very detailed master calendar in order to keep track of the specific dates in each segment of the football year when specific responsibilities must be met. At the start of each year I review the past year's calendar and make any modifications that are necessary to improve our program. Consequently, I am able to know what activities are coming up in the next week or the next month, based on what we have done in the past. As you can tell, I am a believer in routine. I think that it is important to maintain consistency in what you do. In addition to the calendar, I keep a very detailed written record of what is going on in the program. I keep spiral notebooks on each segment of the program. These notes include my thoughts about what is working well and where adjustments need to be made.

Nothing that we do is accidental. I have a staff meeting every morning at 8:00 AM and one every afternoon at 1:00 PM. Everything that occurred in past staff meetings is documented. The agenda for each staff meeting is developed from the previous year's meeting. For example, at the first staff meeting of our summer program I can look back at the previous summer's meeting notes and create the new agenda. We have a staff meeting on the Monday after we finish spring practice. It's just routine for us. Prior to this meeting I will go back and look at the agendas for the last three or four years to make sure that I am going to get everything covered. Between the calendars and the notebooks, virtually everything we do is recorded for future evaluation and modification.

Coach Kramer noticed Snyder's attention to detail from his first interactions with him. "No one was ever hired as a head coach, at any time, or any place, that is more prepared than Bill Snyder. He knows what size paper clips are used. He knows what the custodian is doing. He is ahead of everybody. He knows everything going on in the program — everything."

This attention to detail is noticed by parents who visit with Coach Snyder during the recruiting process One parent remarked, "We were impressed by the fact that they were so organized, so detailed, so precise. Everything was just so professional."

The attention to detail continues to the practice field. Tom Byers recalls that he "always wondered what Snyder had to say as he talked into his tape recorder during practices. Every day at practice he would carry it with him and record his thoughts. You would be surprised how many of us went out and bought a recorder for our classes in college."

According to Kevin Lockett, "If you looked at one of his practice schedules you would see drills going from 2:30 to 2:41 and then from 2:42 to 2:47. That aspect is passed on to his coaches and his players. That is why the program has been so successful for the past five or six years. He pays attention to the smallest details. That is one of the things that makes him one of the very best coaches in the country."

Coach Snyder pays attention to details because every detail is important. Greg Sharpe remembers his interview with Coach Snyder prior to being offered the position as the "Voice of the Wildcats." "Before I was offered the job Coach Snyder wanted to meet with me. He wanted to talk with me to find out what my thoughts were on various topics. He wanted to know how I would handle certain situations. It was clear that if I was going to do this job I was expected to make sure every detail was in place."

A Leader Must See the Big Picture

When we talked with Coach Snyder about his organizational skills, we were particularly interested in how he was able to overhaul an entire culture and at the same time pay attention to small details. *I am concerned about everything that impacts our program, with the entirety of our program. The head coach or the CEO is the person who is supposed to be concerned with how every particular thing impacts the total program. Consequently, there are few people who are in a position to see the big picture. By not seeing the whole picture, it may mean that you might make decisions that are not in the best interests of the whole program. I delegate a great deal of responsibility. I want the offensive and defensive coordina-*

tors to be looking out for their respective parts of the program. And I want the various position coaches to be focusing on their responsibilities. Everybody has a very prominent part and role that's inter-related to the whole program. However, that doesn't mean that a decision made by one of my coaches, that may be best for his particular area is necessarily going to be a positive decision for the entire program. Consequently, it becomes important for me, as it would be for anyone in the same role, to make sure that I have all of the information available. This ensures that decisions that are made at the subordinate level are decisions that I have had a chance to review before there is a final stamp on it. I must always keep in mind that individual decisions, even though positive in one hemisphere, have to be positive as they relate to everything that is going on.

This ability to delegate authority, while at the same time coordinating decision making is understood by those who work closely with him. Greg Sharpe describes the process: "He delegates, but checks up on those he has entrusted tasks to. For example, he will ask his coordinators, 'Do we know want we are going to do on fourth and short on the goal line?' He will ask the pertinent questions so that he knows what they are doing at a critical time, but he lets them pretty much lay everything else out. He lets them do their jobs, until that critical moment when the Head Coach must make a decision."

In addition to focusing on details, consistency is another hallmark of Coach Snyder's style. Coach Kramer recalls that, "Snyder not only raises the standard of what is expected, but his standards are consistent. Every day you meet at 8:00 and 1:00, not 8:01 or 1:01." According to Kramer, Snyder's attention to detail is not a new phenomenon. "In 1974 Snyder was going to every clinic he could get to. At the clinics, he sat in the the front row and took notes. He would then go back to his room, reread his notes, and annotate them. He is absolutely in the top tier of coaching in the country, and he's is not slowing down."

Leadership Lesson Number Twenty

Managing time, stress, and emotions are learnable leadership skills. The need for these skills increases as the demands of leadership increase.

The need to manage priorities, time, stress, and emotions increases as the demands of the leadership position increase. Just putting in the time is not enough, you must be able to make the best use of the time that you have. The intricacies of day-to-day management of time, stress, and emotions are often the hidden side of leadership. When we asked Coach Snyder to talk about how he manages his time, he shared the following specific strategies.

I go through the same process of establishing values that I ask our players to use, and our lists are very similar because what is important to them is important to me. Outside of my faith and family, my priority is to do what I can to develop the best possible football team, and to help direct youngsters to become the best people that they can become, and to help guide them to become the best students they can become. Those same priorities carry over to my family and to my own children.

Honest Self-Assessment is Essential for Success

On a day-to-day basis, Coach Snyder evaluates his own progress toward his goals. He is a firm believer in self-assessment. *Self-assessment is essential in order to determine progress. This assessment is not based on what the newspaper prints, not what I believe someone else thinks, or not what someone else says they think. My self-assessment is based on what I actually know about myself, and whether or not I am sticking with the process. If I am, there will be measurable results. As far as establishing my criteria of my progress, I evaluate myself based upon the accomplishments of others. However, as I tell our players, "it must be an honest self-assessment." There is a natural tendency to assess ourselves in the most positive light, and sometimes we might not be honest or realistic in how we see ourselves. However this lack of honesty will interfere with gaining useful information upon which to make decisions.*

Coach Snyder keeps a journal which contains a record of what he did each day and how he felt about what he did. *Although there are times when it is not complete, I attempt to write in it each day. I am pretty good about that in this respect because this job, like so many others, is so complex and has so many segments. I need to keep a great deal of material well organized. For example, my diary, or journal, is organized around the natural time frame of my responsibilities. There are segments that cover spring football, our summer program, the actual football season, the recruiting season, and the out-of-season program.*

My days are scheduled around the segment of the season we are in. My work schedule is different in each of the four or five segments. For example, during the course of the season, I get to the office at 7:30 AM and I formulate or finalize the agenda for our 8:00 AM staff meeting. We meet at 8:00 AM. We have a variety of specific topics and areas of the program that we cover each day. The same general categories and topics are covered during the same segments every year. The middle of the morning is divided between meetings with our staff — meeting with our offensive coaches, and meeting with our defensive coaches. Late in the morning, I attend to mail and any correspondence that needs to be taken care of.

I schedule non-team related meetings over the lunch hour. I do this for two reasons: one is because I don't eat lunch so that gives me an opportunity to meet with people outside of our regular schedule during the day, and secondly most people have to be pretty serious about wanting to have a meeting if they are going to give up their lunch hour to do it. This gives me some confidence that there is a good reason for the meeting. We have a second regularly scheduled staff meeting at 1:00 PM. Like our morning meetings, there is a general schedule of material to be covered on each day. During the rest of the afternoon, I watch videotapes of various opponents. Late in the afternoon we have our meetings with our players. Practice starts at 4:00 PM each day.

Coach Snyder is a hands-on leader; he wants direct feedback regarding the progress of each player as well as the opportunity to reinforce the progress that each player is making. *After each practice I ask all coaches to visit with players in the locker room. During this time we address any issues that come up and solve any problems that have surfaced at practice. We also use this time to ensure that each player has a positive attitude before he leaves the locker room. A positive word to someone who has had a bad practice or to someone who is a third or fourth team player helps them understand that they are very significant to the program. It is very important to us that everyone leave in a positive frame of mind.*

After practice I come back to the office and review all of the practice tapes. We videotape everything that goes on in all the different segments of practice. Obviously, it is impossible to see nine or ten different activities that are going on simultaneously, so the tapes allow me to see everything that took place. I spend the evenings making preparation for the things that are important for the different segments of the practice. During the season the other coaches and I will be here until midnight or later.

The impact of Coach Snyder's time management, focus, and modeling can be observed in the conduct of his players. Doug Beisel, the father of a current player, states, "My son is learning discipline every day. Day in and day out, the players experience a very well-organized schedule. They clearly understand that there will be consequences for not being on time. Consequently, they become more disciplined, more organized, and more goal-oriented than they were prior to leaving home."

Student life can be stressful. What suggestions do you have for handling stress?

Peggy Niemann
Class of '98, Nortonville, Kansas

Daily Planning: Establish priorities daily; address them in order of importance; stay with it until completed or solved; allow enough time to complete each task; don't schedule more than you can complete; stay on schedule; allow additional time in schedule if necessary; and schedule breaks and exercise time.

Coach Snyder

Although managing time and being able to set priorities are very important, leaders must also be able to manage stress. Over a period of time, Coach Snyder has developed habits that allow him to put in the hours that he does, while at the same time staying focused and managing stress. Clearly, maintaining a good sense of humor helps. When we asked him how he does it, he joked, *How well I have handled stress may be another story. I am really only 35 years old, I just look older! Although there is a lot of stress involved with coaching, there are many, many other profes-*

sions that are at least as stressful. *I need a pretty even keel to perform at the level that I wish to. However, there are some sacrifices that come with being on an even keel. I probably can't enjoy the highlights, the high points, the tip of the mountain, as much as maybe I would like to. However, that is the sacrifice you make not to suffer the consequences or depth of despair that others may experience. This does not mean that I do not experience joy or disappointment, but it is within a manageable range.*

Although I have not experienced every situation in the country, I do think that the situation I found when I got here was pretty unique. If you are someone who rides the the roller coaster of emotion, I don't think you could survive in this profession over an extended period of time. I tell the young folks, there will be no more Joe Paternos or Tom Osbornes, there are no more Bear Bryants. There are no more people who are going to sit at the head coaching desk for an extended period of time; the demands are too great, the stress can be too great over a long period of time. If you get into the profession as a head coach too young, it will wear you out before your time. You better plan on having two or three professions, or career fields.

In the corner of Coach Snyder's office is a stair climber. When asked if he uses it, he replied, *I do use it. I incorporate it into my time management program. I'm not opposed to exercise, in fact I enjoy it. I love it to a certain degree because I was active as a youngster and was brought up in sports. Exercise has been a big part of my life that I enjoy. But, exercise can interfere with your time schedule. It interferes with mine, so I have the exercise machine in my office so that I can watch game tapes while I get some exercise at the same time.*

When Coach Snyder is in the process of selecting staff, he looks at how well they handle stress and their emotions. *I am not interested in abusive people. I'm not interested in people who demonstrate a lack of restraint. I am interested in people who are genuinely concerned about young people. I am interested in people who have the organizational skills to manage the kind of demands that I am going to place upon them. I'm not as interested in what in this profession, is termed X's and O's people as much as I am those who have a strong belief and basic fundamental approach to whatever their position would be teaching fundamentals of the game of football.*

I believe in promoting from within whenever it is at all possible. For example, Michael Smith has been a very important person in our program.

He has been in the program and understands all facets of it. He under-stands and is committed to our values and goals. He understands the process that we follow. As long as they are good people and have a strong feeling about young people we believe they can make a significant positive contribution.

Dennis Mullin reflects, "In business, if you let your critics guide you instead of focusing on your job, it will result in your stress level getting way out of kilter. Bill's total concentration on his job allows him to manage stress better than the average person. I think he has an outstanding ability to prioritize. A lot of leaders, myself included, are not very good at organizing and prioritizing. Bill has the ability to says 'yes' to the things that are important in his life, and is able to keep focused on the things that are important to him."

There is no question that Coach Snyder demands a great deal from himself and from everyone in the program. In some organizations, high expectations are often accompanied by very high levels of stress. This stress is sometimes translated into shouting and ranting. Bob Snell has noted, however, "If I were working under the stress that he operates in, I'm not sure that I would be able to avoid lashing out at someone. Yet, he doesn't to do that. He always appears to be serene and rational. On the sideline he may pace a little faster, but he's not throwing things, and we've had coaches who were."

This is not to imply that Coach Snyder has never shown emotion. However, even in those situations he is quick to regain his focus. As Jim Epps observes, "I have seen him angry to the point that he will cuss, and then he will apologize. He makes it absolutely clear that he is not angry at the individual, but is upset by the situation. You have to realize that most coaches could teach sailors how to cuss. But, with him, there is a certain decorum. If that ever breaks, even for a moment, he will quickly apologize and make it right."

His ability to keep his calm when in the midst of what may seem to an outsider as chaos, is based partially on his attention to detail. One of the reasons that he does not panic is because he is so well prepared. Stan Weber gives the following example. "Coach Snyder expects the coaches in the press box to be so well prepared that in every situation they are selecting from the three most appropriate plays for that situation. The great leaders like Snyder have trained themselves not to get emotional in pressure situations. He has taught himself to focus on the plan."

Greg Sharpe observes that, "One of the things that his players appreciate the most about him is how solid he is. He does not get rattled. He handles every situation the same way. He handles a loss the same way he handles a win. After a loss, he says, 'OK you did not win today, but I still have faith in you. I still have confidence in you.'"

Theoretical Context

As is evident in this chapter, Coach Snyder possesses an exceptional ability to competently manage details, time, and priorities. Perhaps not as evident, but equally impressive, is his ability to handle stress and emotions. In his book, *Emotional Intelligence*, D. P. Goleman writes of the importance of positively managing emotions; i.e., that successful emotional management is equated with success. Mergerian, in her article "An Affair of the Heart: Emotional Intelligence and Transformational Leadership," finds that there is an important and significant relationship between transformational leadership and emotional intelligence.

Coach Snyder's ability to manage stress so well, regardless of the pressure, is evidenced by the fact that he does not lose control of his emotions in a way that negatively impacts others. We find this remarkable, particularly in the confrontational culture of football. Just as the search committee was initially impressed with Coach Snyder's civility, we are continually impressed with the fact that he insists upon civility from himself and from others.

For further information about day-to-day management we recommend:

Bolman, L. G., and Deal, T. E. (1995). *Leading with Soul: An Uncommon Journey of Spirit.* San Francisco: Jossey-Bass.

Covey, S. R. (1994). *First Things First.* New York: Simon and Schuster.

Gardner, J. W. (1981). *Self-Renewal.* New York: Norton.

Goleman, D. P. (1997). *Emotional Intelligence.* New York: Bantam Books.

Hesselbein, F., Goldsmith, M., and Beckhard, R. (1996). *The Leader of the Future: New Visions, Strategies, and Practices for the Next Era.* San Francisco: Jossey-Bass.

Mergerian, L. E.(1996) "An Affair of the Heart: Emotional Intelligence and Transformational Leadership," *Journal of Leadership Studies*, 3 (3), 313-48.

Epilogue

HEN WE APPROACHED Coach Snyder with the proposal for his book, we had two concerns. First, we were apprehensive that he would either be too busy, or not be interested in the project. This concern was quickly allayed. As soon as we told him that the book would be used as a supplemental text in the Leadership Studies program, and that all profits would benefit Kansas State University students, he agreed to the collaboration. Our second concern was more personal. We have been teaching and doing research in the area of leadership for 20 years. In that time we have developed strong beliefs about leadership. We were not sure what we would do if we discovered that Coach Snyder's leadership philosophy was not compatible with ours. Intuitively we believed that Coach Snyder was competent, ethical, caring, and knowledgeable. However, we had little personal knowledge about what he believed. All that we knew for sure was that whatever it was that he was doing seemed to be working. In this age of cynicism, "spin doctors," dishonesty, and manipulation, we share some of society's skepticism.

Our second concern was dispelled during our first extended interview.

You will recall in our discussion about storytelling that we spoke about Coach Snyder's affinity for the story of *Pinocchio*. As we listened to him talk about why this story meant so much to him, and about his desire to help young people find their way to adulthood, we knew that we were in the presence of an extraordinarily honest, compassionate, and dedicated individual. As he talked about his approach to leadership, we found ourselves nodding our heads in agreement, and pointing out that much of what he is doing in the football program is very consistent with what we are teaching in the Leadership Studies program. Additionally, he continually presented us with original and extremely interesting ideas. What is most impressive to us was the fact that Coach Snyder's actions and his words are seamless. We were encouraged to see that integrity, commitment, and honesty can actually coexist with success.

Our conversations with Coach Snyder served as the organizer for the material. His philosophy, what he calls "just common sense," is very compatible with the best of transformational leadership. For example, the transforming leader is morally uplifting. Bernard Bass, in his 1996 article "The Ethics of Transformational Leadership," states that leaders can be described as transformational when they "increase awareness of what is right, good, important, and beautiful, when they help to elevate followers' needs for achievement and self-actualization, when they foster in followers higher moral maturity, and when they move followers to go beyond their self-interests for the good of their group, organization, or society." Coach Snyder is committed to the following transformational principles. Bill Snyder:

- believes that people are basically good,
- demonstrates delegation of responsibility,
- is trustworthy and trusting of his associates,
- enhances self-worth and self-respect of his staff and players,
- minimizes status differences between players,
- has a walk-around, hands-on style of management,
- places a high priority on developing self and others to full potential,
- believes that as the organization succeeds, the individual will succeed,
- is committed to aligning the individual and organizational goals,

- leads by example,
- is an inspiring motivator,
- provides strong intellectual stimulation,
- avoids manipulation and coercion,
- establishes goals that are value-based, and
- models emotional maturity.

When many people think about leadership, they think of the capacity to take charge and get things done. This view keeps some from focusing on the importance of teamwork. The leadership lessons that we have presented focus on thinking about the individual and his or her goals as well as the goals of the organization.

The complexity of the football program mirrors the complexity of today's business tasks. Both demand that the participants be capable of engaging difficult problems independently, and yet within the vision of the organization. Developing such participants requires leaders and followers with high levels of both skill and will. Leadership is not just having the power to make decisions; rather, it is finding a way to be successful in collaboratively defining the essential purpose of the organization, and then empowering the entire organization to become energized and focused. When such a focus has been achieved, the leadership process becomes transformative for everyone.

Coach Snyder's style of leading not only results in a high level of goal achievement, it also has very positive effects on the development of followers, as indicated by the motivation, commitment, and cohesiveness of the people in his program. Throughout this book, we presented the voices of his followers as documentation that Coach Snyder's use of transformational leadership makes a difference in the lives of all those who participate in the process. We have enjoyed the process of writing this book. Thanks for joining us.

Our Challenge to the Reader

We began this book by listing our underlying assumptions. The first is that leadership can be taught and learned. If you agree with this assumption we are pleased. If you have learned more about leadership from Coach Snyder's lessons, we are even more pleased. But what is most important is the translation of these ideas into your personal arena. Our challenge to you is to "finish" the book by taking the next step and applying the *Leadership Lessons from Bill Snyder* to your life.

For further information about leadership:

Bass, B.M. (1996). "The Ethics of Transformational Leadership." 3/24/96 — http://civicsource.org/klsp/klspdocs/bbass

Bass, B.M., (1990). *Bass and Stogdill's Handbook or Leadership: Theory, Research, and Managerial Applications*, 3rd Ed. New York, The Free Press.

Heider, J. (1985). *The Tao of Leadership*. Atlanta: Humanics New Age.